97396

Thorsten Klooster

SMART SURFACES

and their Application in Architecture and Design

with contributions by
Niels Boeing, Simon Davis and Almut Seeger

Birkhäuser
Basel · Boston · Berlin

At first sight, surfaces are boundaries, apparently enclosing the substance of things. The philosophers of the Classical world were aware of the implications of this observation. Rather than being a continuum, they speculated, matter consists of smaller, ultimate units: 'átomos'—a Greek word meaning 'uncuttable', or something that cannot be divided. It took over 2000 years until physicists were able to provide empirical proof of this hypothesis. Their findings were rather more complex than had been suspected by the ancient philosophers. The atoms themselves are composed of different elementary particles: leptons on one hand, constituting the extra-nuclear electrons, and quarks on the other, making up the protons and neutrons forming the atomic nucleus. Niels Bohr's first modern atomic model resembles earlier models of the cosmos—electrons orbiting the atomic nucleus like planets around the sun. The analogy calls to mind 'Powers of Ten', a remarkable science education documentary produced by the designer couple Ray and Charles Eames in 1977. Still fascinating today, the film is structured so as to depict our fundamental scientific understanding of dimension, exemplifying our conception of the interrelationship of cosmos, macrocosm, microcosm and nanospace. "As we draw upon the atom's attracting centre, we enter upon a vast inner space" says the narrator during the fictional flight into the very core of the earth.

As far as the design of objects and spaces is concerned, considerations of surfaces are generally understood to involve a decision about materiality. Yet the subject is rather complex from the point of view of design and architecture, the required know-how including both objective and subjective categories, 'technical knowledge' as well as 'experience'—the result of a process incorporating a great number of considerations. To understand a material properly, it is necessary to know about its scientifically established properties and the industrial fabrication or processing techniques and workmanship involved, as well as developing a familiarity with how the material feels and looks, which may necessitate delving into its history or traditional and regional usage. The properties and usability of a material cannot be assessed satisfactorily on the basis of its technical specifications alone; usable 'material parameters' are generally established when a communication between development, technology and design takes place, elucidating individual approaches to and experiences with the material. The different areas involved in the design process vary, however, in respect of their openness to dialogue. The building industry, in particular, has often profited from material and process engineering innovations made in other disciplines. While more scope in product design may be demanded at times, fundamental technological innovations are rarely developed in the building industry, which tends to follow the principles of the recognised rules of architecture, preferring to use standards, guidelines, techniques and material categories that have been used successfully for decades or even centuries, and which consequently have hardly changed at all.

The term 'surface' is significant in technical research as well as design, a fact that allows important, yet disparate content to be linked. This versatility makes the word particularly useful for discussing the application to design of a broad spectrum of current developments in other disciplines (mainly outside the design field) focussed on in this publication. Following the route traced by Ray and Charles Eames, an abundance of ground-breaking potential can be found between the 'dimensions' of macro and nano, which can only be described inadequately in terms of material, form and construction. From a physical point of view, the 100 nanometre limit, at which the fundamental physical laws of the macro world appear to change completely, is more important than any superficial limits with which we can interact directly through sensory perception. Material technology research is concerned with what it simply calls the 'function' of a surface. NANO Discourse 3, p. 70 This could, for instance, be a protective function, but could also refer to an energy-generating function, or to light-generating or information-providing surfaces. Precisely this informs the structure of this book, which deals with the areas of Nano, Energy, Light, Climate and Information.

These five terms also allow technological characteristics to be ordered in a meaningful manner, while describing the prospects of modern applications in both research and design. This congruence gives rise to design strategies appropriate for 'surfaces'. A consideration of surfaces permits inclusion of the term 'skin', together with the principles, material concepts and philosophies on which it is based (from the point of view of engineering science, building construction and design). SURFACE Discourse, p. 62 With this book, the authors hope to encourage the design of new skins. Creative planning and design should focus more than ever on the areas of design that could be derived from the new technologies. The question of whether and how the technical innovations already available, or promised, will establish themselves also depends to a considerable extent on architects and designers. It is up to them to decide whether their designs will take advantage of the greater number of options and alternatives available to users.

Arthur C. Clarke, 2001 — A Space Odyssey, p. 216
The thing's hollow—it goes on forever—and—oh my God—it's *full of stars!*

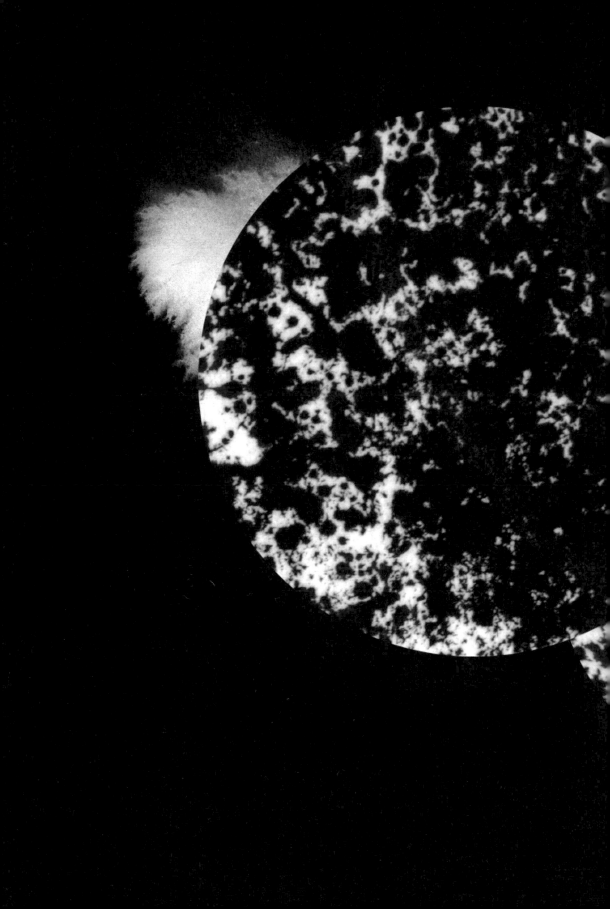

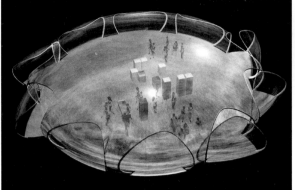

ill. Surfaces.08.1, ill. Surfaces.08.2
**Manifesto of technology transfer. The experimental building
R129 (Werner Sobek) is influenced by automotive design
and aerospace technology.**
• See Surfaces.08, p. 174

ill. Energy.10.1, ill. Energy.10.2
**The *Algae Balloons* by 202 Collaborative turn around the principle of pot and plant.
Stimulated by sunlight, energy algae living in the 'pot' underneath the balloon produce
hydrogen which is captured in the transparent elastic envelopes.**

ill. Information.01.1, ill. Information.01.2
The *Blubber Bots* by Jed Berg explore abstract
principles of the network-based communication
of information. The friendly, zeppelin-like
Bots react to light impulses and detected mobile
phone signals.
• See Information.01, p. 162

ill. Nano.04.1
Water droplets on a super-hydrophobic
(nanostructured) surface.
(Stefan Seeger, University of Zurich)
• See Nano.04, p. 166

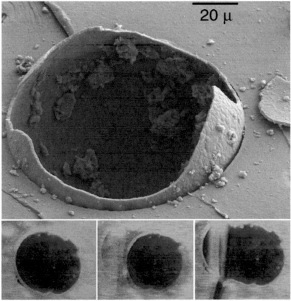

ill. Nano.06.1, ill. Nano.06.2
Damaged, self-healing, nanoscale polymer capsule
(E. Brown and N. Sottos, University of Illinois).
The repairing agent is released when the material matrix
is subjected to torsion.

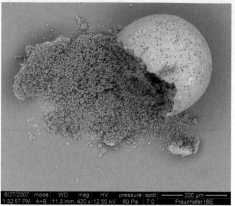

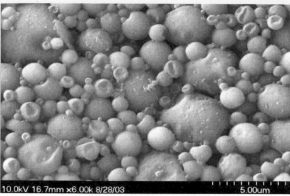

ill. Climate.11.1
Micro-encapsulated latent heat storage PCM
(Fraunhofer ISE).

ill. Climate.12.1
PCM in gypsum plaster (Fraunhofer ISE).

ill. Information.13.1, ill. Information.13.2
Conductive *e-skin matrix* (Takao Somea and Tsuyoshi Sekitani, University
of Tokyo). The material combines the conductivity of metal with the elasticity
of rubber. It can either be used for energy transmission, or as an artificial
skin able to register pressure and heat.

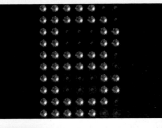

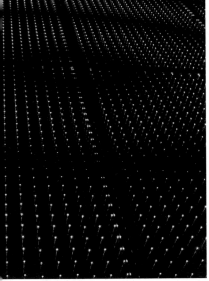

ill. Information.04.1, ill. Information.04.2
Mediaballs—Christian Rothe and Kay Michalczack.
Low-cost, media façade system, based on
table tennis balls, for the display of scrolling text.
• See Information.04, p. 170

ill. Light.06.1
Laminated glass with integrated LEDs.
The diodes, embedded in transparent cast resin, can be controlled
individually via invisible conductors
along the inner glass surface.

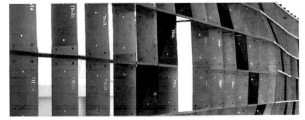

ill. Surfaces.12.1
Wall construction of laser-cut, angled sheet metal using CAAM
(CAAD Blech, ETH Zurich).

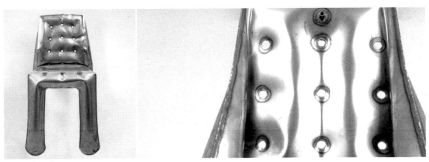

ill. Surfaces.04.01, ill. Surfaces.04.02
Objects created through hydraulic pressure using the *FIDU method*
developed by Oskar Zieta. The method produces a formal language
not previously associated with sheet metal.
• See Surfaces.04, p. 166

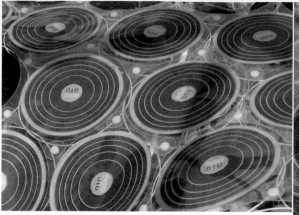

ill. Energy.11.1, ill. Energy.11.2, ill. Energy.11.3, ill. Energy.11.4
Laminated foil matrix bearing circular polymer solar
cells (dye-sensitized solar cells) in combination with LED lights,
by Loop.pH.

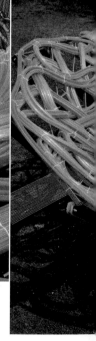

ill. Climate.02.1, ill. Climate.02.2, ill. Climate.02.3
Architectural installation *BAD*, by Smaq. An absorber woven of 1,000 m of hose captures sunlight to
heat up the bath water.
• See Climate.02, p. 161

ill. Energy.12.1
'Power Plastic'. Thin-film solar cell
in the form of a flexible strip.

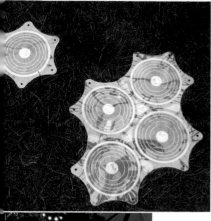

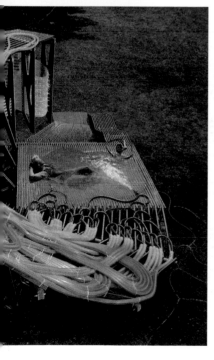

ill. Climate.09.1
Biological Habitat, Form 090704, by Zbigniew Oksiuta (Architecture Biennale, Venice 2004). Globular object after molecular deformation and invagination, diameter approx. 2 m, gelatine, of grade 270° Bloom. Taste & smell: neutral. Oksiuta's *Spatium Gelatum* is an example of design by morphogenesis.
ill. Climate.09.2
Transgenic object, vegetal callus culture (callus: a complex of undiffe-rentiated, totipotent cells). The space-enclosing structures of *Spatium Gelatum* are used by *Breeding Spaces* to grow three-dimensional vegetal constructions.
• See Climate.09, p. 176

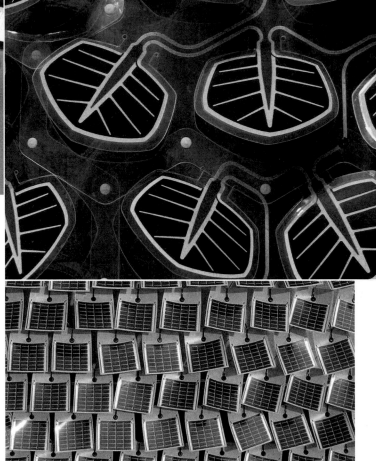

ill. Energy.04.1, ill. Energy.04.2,
ill. Energy.04.3
Hybrid energy generation system
Grow **by SMIT. Thin-film solar
modules (solar leaves), suspended
on piezoelectrical actuators,
convert solar and wind energy into
electrical power.**
• See Energy.04, p.168

ill. Information.14.1
**Construction variant of an Arduino
board. The open-source hardware
platform is used in art and design.**

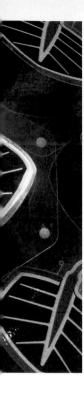

ill. Information.11.1, ill. Information.11.2, ill. Information.11.3
The *Waterradio* by Clemens Winkler combines the aesthetic of the natural with the capacities of the technical to create a new synthesis of surface intelligence.
• See Information.11, p.178

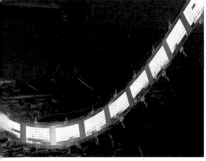

ill. Nano.07.1
Nanopaper battery by R. Linhardt (Rensselaer). Material made of cellulose fibres and small quantities of nanotubes.

ill. Nano.08.1
Metamaterial that has a negative refractive index, by David Smith (Duke University). The electromagnetic refraction behaviour of such materials is different from that normally occurring in nature. This metamaterial coating is a step towards the 'cloak-of-invisibility' effect.

ill. Light.07.1
Roll-to-roll organic LED. OLEDs, which can be described as light emitting plastics, are seen as the lighting technology of the future.

ill. Nano.09.1, ill. Nano.09.2
Self-healing polymer, by Kathleen Toohey and Nancy Sottos (University of Illinois). Cracks in the plastic coating are sealed by a polymer that emerges, at the site of damage, from a micro-channel system integrated in the substrate.

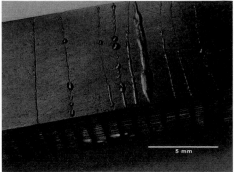

ill. Light.04.1, ill. Light.04.2, ill. Light.04.3
GreenPix—Zero Energy Media Wall by Simone Giostra & Partner with Ove Arup. LED media façade with integrated solar panels. The electricity required to operate the LEDs at night is generated by converting sunlight during the day.
• See Light.04, p.168

ill. Energy.13.1, ill. Energy.13.2
Smart Wrap (patent pending) by Kieran Timberlake investigates the idea of an off-the-roll material consisting of OLED (light), PCM (climate) and flexible solar modules (energy), continuously manufactured using combined lamination and printing processes, which combines all the important functions of a building envelope.

ill. Information.15.1
Touchscreen interface for controlling the building functions of a *Smart Home*.

ill. Nano.10.1, ill. Nano.10.2, ill. Nano.10.3
Functional coatings produced with the aid of nanotechnological thin-film processes.
Photocatalytic cleaning coatings (easy-to-clean, anti-mist).
Antireflective coating on the glass covers of solar modules reduce the energy loss
from reflected solar radiation.

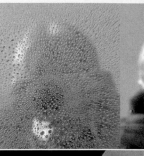

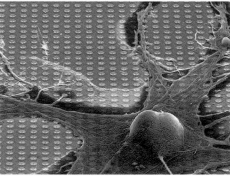

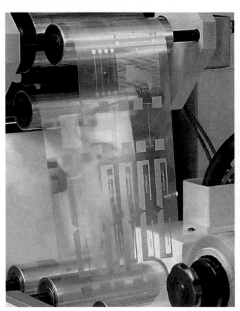

ill. Information.16.1
Sensor array of a neurochip. 16,384 highly sensi-
tive sensors are directly connected with a
living nerve cell and read the electrical activity
of the cell.

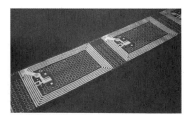

ill. Information.17.1
Printable electronics. Development at present
is focused on the production of RFID
elements, in order to develop the necessary
technical knowledge.

ill. Information.18.1
RFID transponder (transmitter-
responder). Computer chip with
antenna.

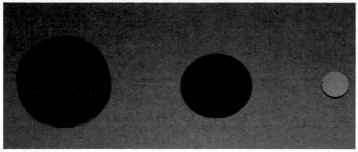

ill. Nano.11.1
'Blackest black', by Shawn-Yu Lin (Rensselaer Institute with Rice University), probably the darkest synthetic material in the world (centre of picture), increases the efficiency of photovoltaic modules and solar thermal absorbers.

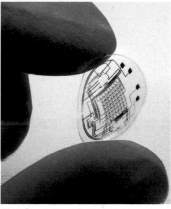

ill. Information.19.1
The prototype *Bionic Contact Lens* (Babak Parviz, University of Washington) demonstrates the potential of Augmented Reality and body-contact information-active surfaces.

ill. Light.08.1, ill. Light.08.2
Vortex. Three-dimensional reflector structure made of polyester fabric, by FAF Design.

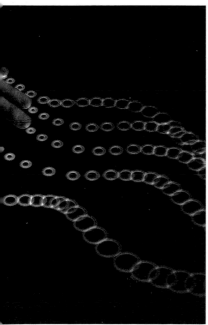

ill. Information.20.1
A multitouch surface by to-fuse (Christian Iten and Emanuel Zgraggen). Platform to develop new intuitive forms of interaction.

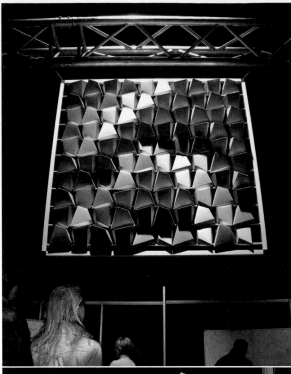

ill. Light.09.1
Printed light.
Electroluminescent film.

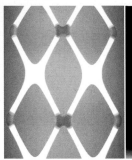

ill. Light.10.1, ill. Light.10.2
Additive light-emitting surface modules.
X-shaped modules composed of plastic. LEDs.

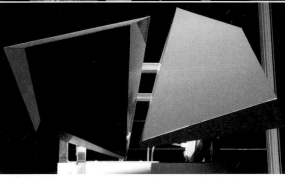

ill. Light.03.1, ill. Light.03.2
Pneumatic media façade *Flare,* by WHITEvoid. Movable
modular metal forms (pixels) reflect the ambient light more or
less strongly, depending on their inclination.
• See Light.03, p.166

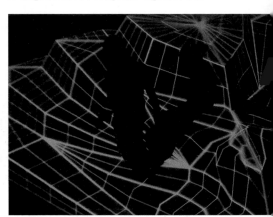

ill. Information.21.1
The complex-shaped *Polygon Playground*
by WHITEvoid provides space for a
maximum of 40 people. Precisely-contoured
dynamic 360° projections react to the
motions of visitors.

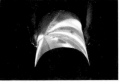

ill. Information.22.1, ill. Information.22.2, ill. Information.22.3
The design study *flicflex,* by Chris Woebken, minimises the graphic interface
and other aids. Different ways of handling information arise from the
minimalist material logic of a flexible display.

ill. Surfaces.07.1, ill. Surfaces.07.2
Light and elastic: the dimensionally stable
envelope of the Conference Centre in Badajoz,
made of 12 km of composite profiles (GRP),
designed by Selgascano.
• See Surfaces.07, p. 173

ill. Light.11.1
Temporary installation *Field of Light*, by Bruce Munro, in the grounds of the *Eden Project*.
11 projectors illuminate 6,000 unpowered glass spheres via optic fibres.

ill. Nano.12.1
Aerogel test. This group of materials holds fifteen records for special material properties.

ill. Light.12.1
Escape route markings using photoluminescent paint.

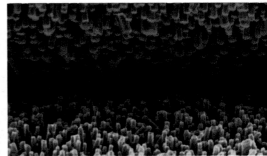

ill. Energy.14.1
Power Shirt by Zhong Lin Wang (GeorgiaTech). Woven into clothing, nano-piezogenerators convert extremely small vibrations (airflows, sound waves or mechanical movements) into electrical energy.

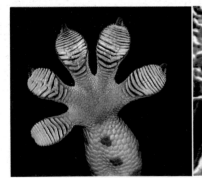

ill. Nano.05.1, ill. Nano.05.2, ill. Nano.05.3
Nanostructured surface by Zhong Lin Wang (Georgia Tech) modelled on a gecko's foot pads. A 3 × 3 cm adhesive strip can support up to 100 kg.
• See Nano.05, p.167

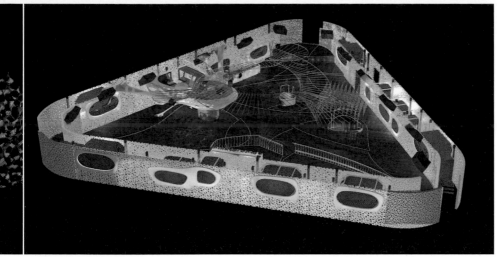

ill. Light.01.1, ill. Light.01.2
The *Cocoon Club* by 3deluxe is conceived as a spatial experimental field in which
othe multi-sensory perception of the room is subject to continuous change,
induced by moving light.
• See Light.01, p. 162

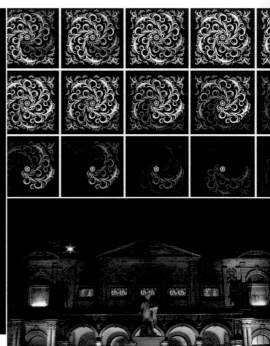

ill. Information.12.1, ill. Information.12.2, ill. Information.12.3
Weather Patterns by Loop.ph. The pattern on the electroluminescence film, printed using a conductive paste, is animated
via 8 to 16 paths.
• See Information.12, p. 179

ill. Nano.13.1
Cross-section of a nanotower (made of carbon nanotubes) from a 3D solar cell (Jud Ready, Georgia Tech). The surface maximisation achieved by the three-dimensional structure increases the energy yield of the module.

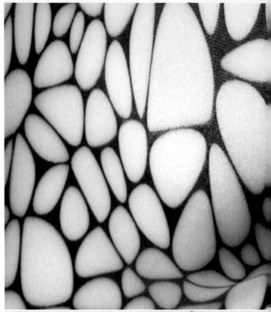

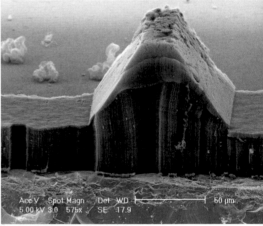

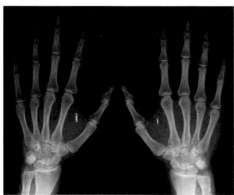

ill. Information.23.1
The RFID implants in Amal Graafstra's hands are programmed to function as keys. He uses them to open his front door, his car door and to log into his computer.

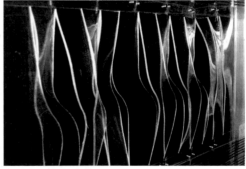

ill. Climate.06.1
The climate control system *Living Glass*, by The Living, measures the carbon dioxide content of the room air. Actuator-controlled gills in the transparent silicone membrane regulate the inflow of fresh air.
• See Climate.06, p.169

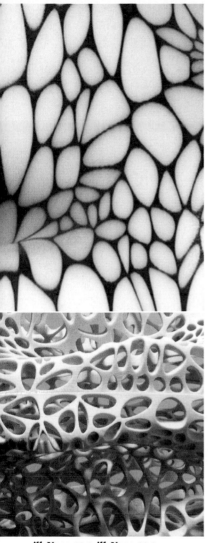

ill. Nano.03.1, ill. Nano.03.2,
ill. Nano.03.3
Construction in Vivo, Neri Oxman with
John Hart. Prototype material
architecture of a partially transparent envelope, created from nanotubes
(CNTs) and polymers, which behaves
like a biomembrane.
• See Nano.03, p.163

ill. Information.10.1, ill. Information.10.2
Sketch Furniture by Front. The traces of lines drawn in the air are trans-
formed into real objects through Motion Capture and Rapid Prototyping.
• See Information.10, p.176

ill. Light.02.1, ill. Light.02.2, ill. Light.02.3
Communicative Lighting Façade (Eastern Façade) of the Center of Contemporary Art
in Cordoba, by Nieto Sobejano Architects with Realities United. During the day,
the sun creates a shadowplay on the relief structure. At night, polygonal depressions
become indirectly illuminated pixels.
• See Light.02, p. 163

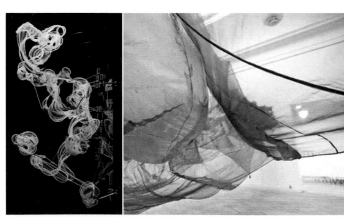

ill. Information.24.1, ill. 24.2
The *Robotic Membranes,* by Mette Ramsgard Thomsen, combine architecture,
textiles technology and robotics. These sensor-actuator-controlled intelligent
membranes demonstrate how information envelopes function.

ill. Energy.15.1, ill. Energy.15.2
The *Integrated Concentrating Dynamic
Solar Façade* (Rensselear CASE)
combines efficient energy generation
with high transparency. Focused
sunlight strikes a stamp-sized semiconductor surface in the centre of the
glass reflector with great intensity.

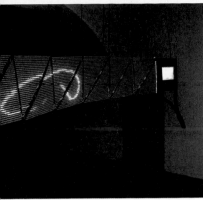

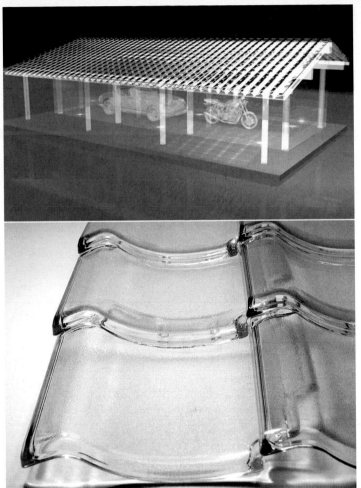

ill. Information.02.1
Echologue by Orkan Telhan. Technical, visual and geometrical spatial abstraction induces socially communicative acts in a public space.
• See Information.02, p. 164

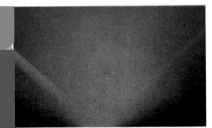

ill. Nano.14.1, ill. Nano.14.2
Thin interference coatings (nano thin film) on metal reflectors increase the efficiency of light guidance systems and lamps by 10 to 20 percent.

ill. Surfaces.13.1, ill. Surfaces.13.2
Transparent Kura, by Tokujin Yoshioka, de-ideologises the aesthetic of complete transparency by applying it to all of the elements making up a house.

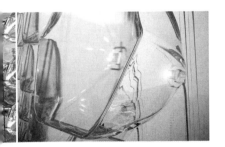

ill. Energy.16.1
Balcony grid of *low-price* micro wind generators by Michael and Dennis Leung (University of Hong Kong). 4 sq.m. can generate 60 per cent of the daily electrical energy requirement.

ill. Light.13.1, ill. Light.13.2, ill. Light.13.3
Detail of the channel structure of a solar thermal absorber, optimised by
means of a surface algorithm.

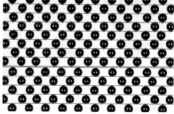

ill. Energy.17.1, ill. Energy.17.2
Semi-transparent, spherical, dye-
sensitive, solar cell.
Tiny spheres absorb sunlight from
all directions.

ill. Light.14.1, ill. Light.14.2
Light guidance system designed for Singapore airport (Bartenbach LichtLabor)
with nanotechnically thin-coated, highly efficient aluminium reflectors.

ill. Light.15.1
Pneumatic actuators move Mark Goulthorpe's *Hyposurface* up or down by up to 60 cm. The surface, which is extremely varied in its motions and highly dynamic, reacts to environmental influences.

ill. Climate.10.1, ill. Climate.10.2
STEMcloud v2.0 by Ecologic Studio is the prototype interactive installation of an 'ecoMachine', conceived as architecture, for breeding oxygen-producing micro-organisms.
• See Climate.10, p. 177

ill. Energy.06.1
Piezotechnical flooring system *Power Leap* by Elizabeth Redmond, which converts pressure impulses into electrical energy.
• See Energy.06, p.173

ill. Surfaces.14.1
Lightweight construction using honeycomb panels: favourable structural properties at low specific weight.

ill. Surfaces.06.1, ill. Surfaces.06.2, ill. Surfaces.06.3
'Elastic space' of the student canteen at Karlsruhe University by J. Mayer H. Architects. The seamless, coloured polyurethane coating gives the surface continuity.
• See Surfaces.06, p.171

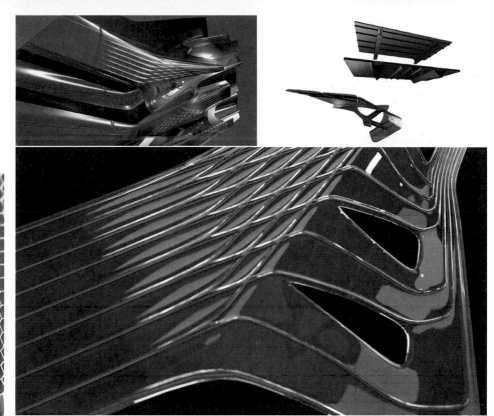

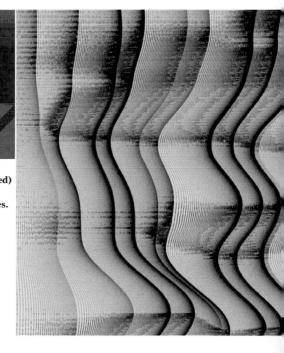

ill. Climate.03.1, ill. Climate.03.2, ill. Climate.03.3
The design study *Bat Wing*, by EMERGENT, is aimed at developing an integrative design logic of envelope, supporting structure and the functions of climate and light, using bioconstructivist techniques.
• See Climate.03, p. 161

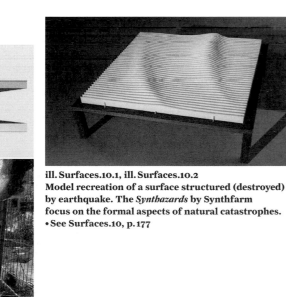

ill. Surfaces.10.1, ill. Surfaces.10.2
Model recreation of a surface structured (destroyed) by earthquake. The *Synthazards* by Synthfarm focus on the formal aspects of natural catastrophes.
• See Surfaces.10, p. 177

ill. Energy.18.1
Different system variants of biomass reactors. Algae convert sunlight into biochemical energy.

ill. Energy.19.1, ill. Energy.19.2
Whereas the electrical energy of solar cells is either consumed directly or has to be stored by complex means, micro-organisms (algae) function, in principle, as a living storage medium for solar energy.

ill. Surfaces.01.1,
ill. Surfaces.01.2
Design study *Adaptive Generative Pattern* by Giorgos Artopoulos and Stanislav Roudavski. Construction of a complex topography using the principles of tesselation (tiling).
• See Surfaces.01, p.160

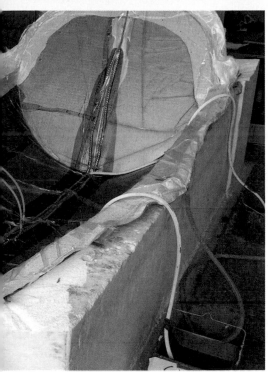

ill. Surfaces.15.1
Structural component made of glass and hybrid fibres in a mould. The utilisation of composite materials makes it possible to create very light, high-strength and complex constructions.

ill. Energy.09.1, ill. Energy.09.2
Urban Battery by MOS. Vertical gardens improve the local climate. Turbines convert warm air flows rising within the glazed structure into electrical energy.
• See Energy.09, p.178

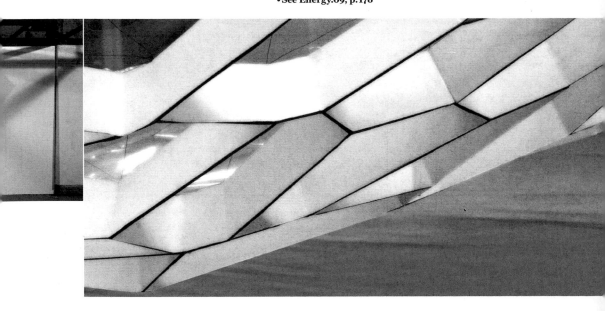

ill. Energy.08.1, ill. Energy.08.2,
ill. Energy.08.3, ill. Energy.08.4
The photovoltaically active curtain of the *Soft House*
(KVA MATx) is made of woven-in thin-film
solar cells. The generation of energy is regulated by
'setting and reefing' the curtains.
• See Energy.08, p. 176

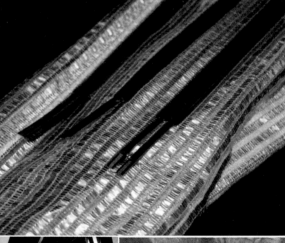

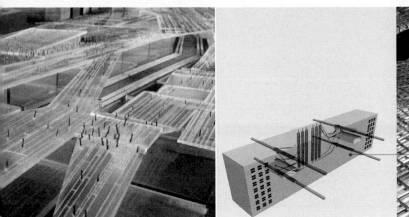

ill. Energy.01.1, ill. Energy.01.2, ill. Energy.01.3
Crowd Farm by James Graham and Thaddeus Jusczyk 'harvests' the kinetic energy of
subway commuters. 30,000 footsteps can supply a subway train with electricity for one second.
• See Energy.01, p.16

ill. Surfaces.09.1, ill. Surfaces.09.2,
ill. Surfaces.09.3, ill. Surfaces.09.4
Sculptures Steg and *Ratiobau* by Heike Klussmann.
The dematerialising effect of light reveals the
aesthetic qualities of Reflexbeton.
• See Surfaces.09, p.175

ill. Energy.20.1
Properties of dye-sensitive cells (Fraunhofer ISE)
such as partial transparency and colouring can
be specifically adjusted. Completely new applications for photovoltaics are conceivable.

ill. Information.25.1, ill. Information.25.2, ill. Information.25.3
Re:orient—*Migrating Architectures* (Re:Orient Team). Wall hangings and
space-forming objects are created from easy-to-manipulate Chinese
children's toys.

ill. Information.08.1, ill. Information.08.2
The Reconfigurable House by Usman Haque and Adam Somlai-Fischer.
The numerous low-tech components of the room installation can
be reconfigured at will by the users.
• See Information.08, p. 174

ill.Information.26.1
Mother 3.2 — Memory of a robotic surrogate by Susanna Hertrich

ill. Energy.05.1, ill. Energy.05.2,
ill. Energy.05.3
Nano Vent Skin by Agustin Otegui.
Semi-transparent bio- and light-
active mesh made of extremely small
micro-turbines and designed to
generate energy from light and wind
on internal and external façades.
• See Energy.05, p. 171

ill. Energy.21.1
Piezoelectric surface
converters can be used
as sensor-actuator
material, or as energy
generators, in surface
building components.

ill. Information.27.1
Nanoscale gyrosensor (position sensor).

ill. Information.03.1
The *Hug-Shirt* by CuteCircuit transmits and
receives hugs. It demonstrates principles of Smart
Clothing and the design of Tangible User
Interfaces (TUI).
• See Information.03, p. 169

ill. Climate.13.1
Detail of multilayer insulation.
The thin, flexible sheeting consists of
several layers of aluminium and
air-enclosing foils.

ill. Information.28.1, ill. Information.28.2, ill. Information.28.3
The *Cassius Lamp*, by Fluidforms. A matrix of 9 × 7 pressure sensors registers punch impulses on the punchbag
and transfers these via an Arduino board to a virtual 3D model which is instantaneously deformed.
The lampshade is generated from the model by means of Rapid Prototyping.

ill. Information.06.1,
ill. Information.06.2
Organic electronics: The *New Sensual
Interfaces* by Chris Woebken permit
new interactive forms of data mining.
• See Information.06, p.172

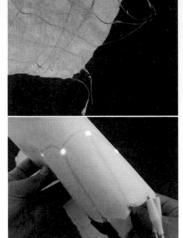

ill. Information.29.1
Full-body Navigation in *Harmony Space:*
The floor projection by e-sense
explores the potential of tangible
user interfaces that involve the whole
body. Chords are produced by a
series of movements around a floor
projection.

ill. Information.07.1,
ill. Information.07.2
Pulp-Based Computing by Marcelo
Coelho and Pattie Maes. The
electrically-conductive composite
material with the properties
of paper can be used in the context of sensor-actuator systems.
• See Information.07, p. 173

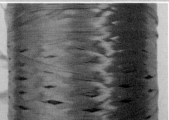

ill. Light.16.1
Large area OLED module by Fraunhofer IPMS.

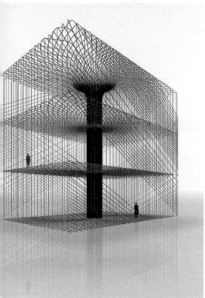

ill. Surfaces.03.1, ill. Surfaces.03.2,
ill. Surfaces.03.3
With *Fiber Architecture*, Tokujin
Yoshioka formulates the vision
of an architecture arising from the
intelligent combination of fibres.
Supporting structure and network
enter into a symbiotic alliance.
• See Surfaces.03, p. 165

ill. Climate.14.1
Satellite with multilayer insulation. MLI foil protects the
equipment against cooling through retroreflection, assists the
uniform distribution of heat and reflects external radiation
to prevent heat gain.

ill. Climate.15.1
Macroencapsulated PCMs in pouches,
metal compartments or dimpled
sheeting allow uncomplicated upgrad-
ing, for example in the form of
suspended cooling ceilings or as
layable roll material.

ill. Information.30.1
The sensor-networked floor registers
a person lying on the ground and
triggers an alarm call.

ill. Energy.22.1
Ink made of nanoparticles should
make it possible to produce
solar cells using printing processes.

ill. Climate.16.1
Cloud by Bouroullec. Polygonal-triangular-structured material elements can be joined together by rubber rings adapted to the system, so as to form room installations of any form.

ill. Light.17.1
Detail of a media façade built out of LED profiles that are woven into a stainless steel network.

ill. Surfaces.16.1, ill. Surfaces.16.2, ill. Surfaces.16.3, ill. Surfaces.16.4
Principles of woven spaces. Installations (principles) *La Pelota* and *MyHome* by Ronan and Erwan Bouroullec.

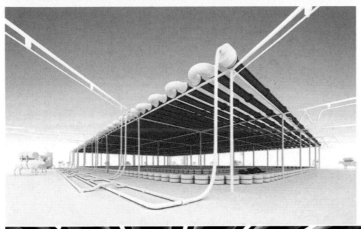

ill. Energy.02.1, ill. Energy.02.2
Design study *Drip Feed* by Thomas Raynaud and Cyrille Berger.
A roof of energy-generating green algae spans the island of Sacca San Mattia near Venice.
• See Energy.02, p. 164

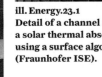

ill. Energy.23.1
Detail of a channel structure from
a solar thermal absorber, optimised
using a surface algorithm
(Fraunhofer ISE).

ill. Energy.24.1
Back contact technology combines higher efficiency with new
possibilities for the design of silicon solar cells. Laser beams
are used to create, in a single step, a delicate metallic meshwork
that conducts electricity.

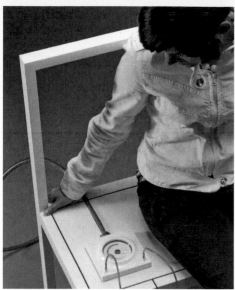

ill. Information.09.1, ill. Information.09.2
The instrumentarium of *Sensillae* (Design: Chris Woebken) creates the framework of an insect-human interaction, using insects as biosensors.
• See Information.09, p. 175

ill. Energy.07.1
Demonstration object *Silent Energy* by Jannis Huelsen, designed to exploit the energy potential of everyday actions by means of piezotechnically activated surfaces.
• See Energy.07, p. 175

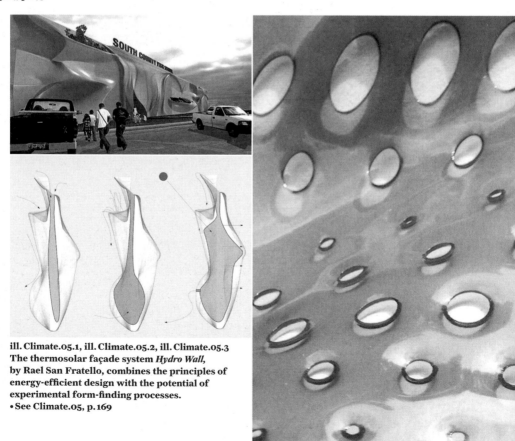

ill. Climate.05.1, ill. Climate.05.2, ill. Climate.05.3
The thermosolar façade system *Hydro Wall*, by Rael San Fratello, combines the principles of energy-efficient design with the potential of experimental form-finding processes.
• See Climate.05, p. 169

Testing of electrically conductive inks made of nanoparticles developed by the Fraunhofer IISB for printed electronic components. The ink adheres less well to the organic insulator (top) than to the surface-treated silicon dioxide (bottom).

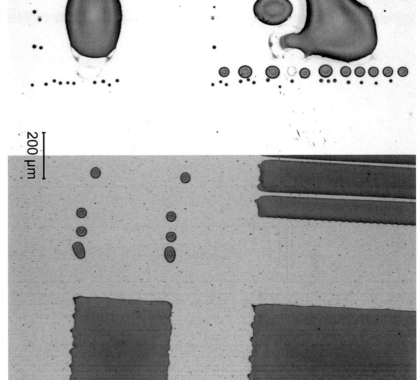

200 μm

ill. Surfaces.11.1, ill. Surfaces.11.2
The Venus Chair (right) in the exhibition *Second Nature* by Tokujin Yoshioka is grown in a tank of water. Crystals form on a matrix of polyester fibres. The synthetic nature of the object demonstrates the aesthetic potential of technological materials.
• See Surfaces.11, p.178

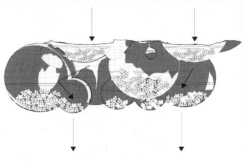

ill. Climate.07.1, ill. Climate.07.2, ill. Climate.07.3
Design study *Massive Skin* by Sven Hansen and
Philipp Thole. Electroluminescent PCM
polymer membrane with the thermal properties
of a massive wall.
• See Climate.07, p. 170

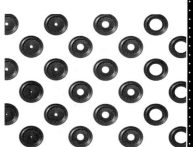

ill. Information.32.1,
ill. Information.32.2
The sensor-actuator controlled
ambient display aperture, by Frédéric Eyl
and Gunnar Green, creates greyscale graphics by controlling ambient
light using a dynamic pixel matrix
of photo lenses.

ill. Nano.02.1
The functional principle of thin films (Lyderic Bocquet): two identical glass balls create very different splash patterns when they come into contact with water. The hydrophilically coated ball enters the water almost without a splash, whereas the hydrophobically nanocoated ball creates a big splash.
• See Nano.02, p. 162

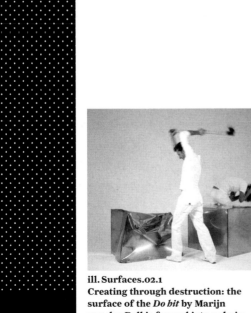

ill. Surfaces.02.1
Creating through destruction: the surface of the *Do hit* by Marijn van der Poll is formed into a chair by hammer blows, according to each user's personal fancy.
• See Surfaces.02, p. 164

ill. Climate.04.1
High Performance Masonry Wall System by Jason Vollen (Rensselaer CASE). The system, consisting of ceramic modules with a special cross section, simulates the climatic response of desert cacti and termite mounds.
• See Climate.04, p. 168

ill. Surfaces.17.1, ill. Surfaces.17.2
Techtile Exhibition 2008 was concerned with tactile design in the context of technical materials. Yasuaki Kakehi, Masashi Nakatani (University of Tokyo) with Nosigner. Using single means (polythene film), the room evokes the elementary feeling of touching ice.

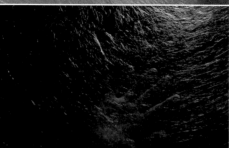

ill. Nano.01.1, ill. Nano.01.2
Light guidance through electrostatically-moved micromirrors, design study by Hartmut Hillmer, University of Kassel. Each mirror (1,000 per cm²) of the *Active Window* is mounted so as to move freely on a kind of leaf spring.
• See Nano.01, p.160

ill. Climate.01.1, ill. Climate.01.2, ill. Climate.01.3, ill. Climate.01.4
Integrating function and insulation in the wall as a building component:
The objects in the installation by Susanne Zottl extend the scope of options in energy-efficient building.
• See Climate.01, p. 161

ill. Climate.01.1, ill. Climate.01.2, ill. Climate.01.3, ill. Climate.01.4
Different designs of vacuum insulation panel (VIP). Innovations are aimed at improving the envelope and core,
the thermal bridges at abutting edges, the variety of formats and form variants of the system, as well as
refining construction design.

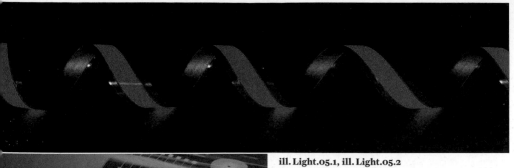

ill. Light.05.1, ill. Light.05.2
Printed electronics. The electroluminiscent foil
combines dynamically illuminated control
elements and current-carrying circuits.
• See Light.05, p. 173

ill. Nano.15.1
Metropolis. Architecture made of
nanotubes by A. John Hart.

ill. Light.18.1
Flexible softlight by Ingo Maurer, made of foil-laminated
OLED elements.

ill. Climate.18.1, ill. Climate.18.2
Thermoactive Building Systems (TABS). Surface components (ceilings and walls) containing hose systems imitate the functional principles of the human organism.

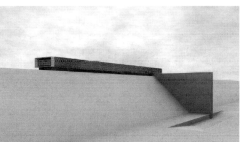

ill. Energy.03.1, ill. Energy.03.2
The *Hydrogen Platform* (designed by Marcel Lehmann) uses different regenerative energy sources (biomass, algae, wind, sun) to produce hydrogen.
• See Energy.03, p. 165

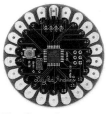

ill. Information.33.1
LilyPad Arduino micro-processor unit for the design of *e-textiles*.

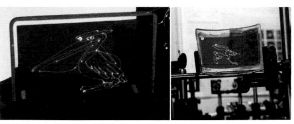

ill. Information.34.1, ill. Information.34.2
Cartoon stills on an optically stimulated, photon upconversion organic display (Tzenka Miteva and Stanislav Balouchev). Animations are played by means of laser diode projection.

ill. Light.19.1
Fluoroscape 2006 by Neil M. Denari Architects. In this spatially and graphically
organised system, distinctions between structural and lighting elements are blurred.

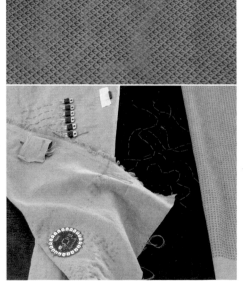

ill. Surfaces.18.1
Design study *P_Wall* by Andrew
Kudless, Matsys.

ill. Surfaces.19.1, ill. Surfaces.19.2
The Interactive Tablecloth by Clemens Winkler
reacts to the pressure of a hand or the warmth
of a cup by changing its surface colour. Impulses
bring about reactions at various points on the
tablecloth, which consists of three textile layers
(pressure sensors, conductive threads and
thermochromic pigments).

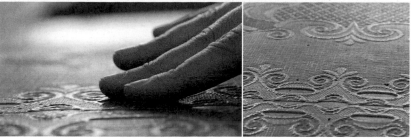

ill. Surfaces.05.1, ill. Surfaces.05.2
Material sample of an ultra high-strength concrete (G.tecz Engineering)
with patterned, structured surface.
• See Surfaces.05, p. 167

ill. Surfaces.20.1
Lightweight construction *Honeycomb Morphologies* by matsys:
favourable structural properties at low specific weight.

ill. Information.35.1,
ill. Information.35.2
Techtile 2 by Nosigner. Continually
generated bubbles illustrate
principles of simplicity and complexity.

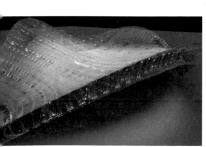

ill. Surfaces.21.1
Vicious Morphologies by Andres
Harris and Onur Ozkaya.
The biomimetic structure resembles
the internal structure of the cranium.

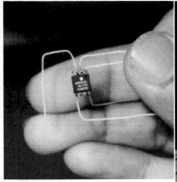

ill. Information.05.1,
ill. Information.05.2
Media House Project—IaaC and MIT
Media Lab: *"The House is the
computer. The Structure is the network."*
• See Information.05, p. 170

ill. Light.20.1
Electroluminescent wallpaper by Jonas Samon.

ill. Climate.19.1
**Wall structure of a thermoactive *Phase Change Material* system
(Fraunhofer ISE).**

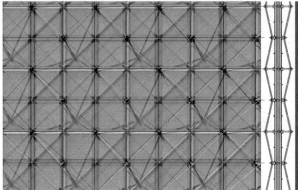

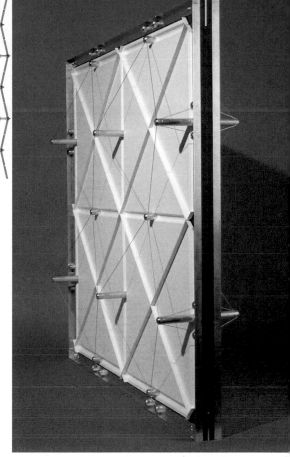

ill. Climate.08.1, ill. Climate.08.2
Non-load-bearing external wall systems with integrated vacuum insulation by Jan Cremers. These very slim, skin-like constructions promise extraordinary insulation values.
• See Climate.08, p.172

ill. Energy.25.1
Thermoelectric generators (TEGs) convert even relatively small temperature differences into electrical energy.

ill. Nano.16.1
Smart Dust. **Clouds of dust-sized sensors create information envelopes around people, objects, rooms, buildings and landscapes.**

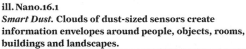

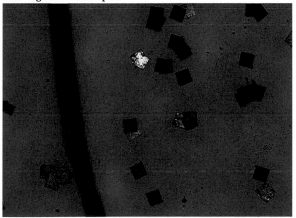

SURFACES Discourse

There is no ready answer to the question of how the intelligence of surfaces is defined. In a short essay, the Italian artist Giuseppe Penone describes his own careful method of working on the industrially manufactured beams that he uses as the starting material for his sculptural work, working away at them with gouger and stylus, layer by layer, following the growth rings, in order to reveal the original form of the young tree trunk: "I went into the woods and wandered along quite slowly, reflectively, noticing with amazement every tiny detail of form."[1] The idea of penetrating the intimacy of the wood using a scalpel, says Penone, into "this history characterised by days of sun, rain and frost, by encounters with insects, animals and other living forms, by accidents, abuse, scoring, cuts, but also by the gentle touch of other plants, can only be born of a sensibility for the material." The genius of Penone's method of working is the reanimation of the material through the cut. The knife, actually the most important tool used for the technological working of wood, defines his artistic relationship with the material. Vivisection, which is what this virtually amounts to, is a fundamental method of scientific research: the investigation of an organism for the purpose of acquiring knowledge. In Penone's case, it is a careful engagement with the external form, and at the same time a personally motivated artistic act of both inquisitive exploration and general demonstration. The purpose of this is to learn more about the formative intelligence of Nature.

The field of research is the first level on which the question posed above can be addressed. The branching in the diagrams used in material science can be read as a genealogy of materials. For a long time, mankind had to get by with a limited number of materials;[2] today the "noble" materials[3] have to compete with a proliferation of young shoots—and it is these that form the basis of this book. At present, materials research has arrived at the molecular level, on which electrostatic natural forces dominate over the forces of gravity and inertia, which are relevant on

1
Penone (1969), Den Wald wiederholen, p. 83.

2
"For about the first million years, there were only about five—wood, rock, bone, horn, and leather—which slowly expanded to include clay, wool, plant fibres, and, relatively recently, metals." See Mazé (2007), Occupying Time, p. 33.

3
"In fact, materials only possess an inherited nobility insofar as they are invested with it by a cultural ideology [...] and this cultural predisposition also tarnishes with time." Baudrillard (1968), System der Dinge [Sytem of Objects], p. 51.

the macro level.[4] Many new materials are therefore determined both by their visual and physical macro properties, as well as by micro and nano scale effects: "Thus the sea change we sense is subtle and subversive because it is occurring below the surface of visible artifacts." Surface has become the technological arena in which both the status quo and the improvement of substances can be represented. The design theorist Ramia Mazé describes the shift in attention from the properties *(appearance)* of a material to the performance of surfaces with allusion to earlier positions: "As structural, chemical and computational properties are integrated at nano-, micro- and macro-scales, even the most traditional material might become dynamic."[5] Along with the Italian material researcher Ezio Manzini, we can speak of a technologisation of materials, which increasingly allows designers to determine their behaviour in advance, rather than simply taking it into account.[6] NANO Discours 1, p. 68 Contrary to earlier assumptions, this advance has not destroyed the hierarchy of substances.[7] On the contrary, it is described as a tendency towards the immaterial, the synthetic, as a result of which the inherent values associated with familiar materials are lost. As a rule, the traditional heritages of synthetic materials (paper, glass, concrete) are thereby overlooked, as is the fact that building materials essentially always represent a specific state of technological knowledge (in the case of wood, that of Antiquity, for example, or in the case of concrete that of the 19th century), for which, with some delay, we develop an understanding that influences our judgment. Part of the fascination of design lies in being able to relate these temporal fragments.[8] ill. Information.11.3, p. 19; Information.11, p. 178 The relationship with technical materials and the possibility of designing smart, intelligent surfaces is not one of juxtaposition, not an 'either/or', but an extension of the scope within which a spontaneous, ill. Surfaces.02.1, p. 51; Surfaces.02, p. 164 artistic or scientific ill. Surfaces.11.1, p. 49; Surfaces.11, p. 178 approach still remains possible, and is required. The walk in the woods corresponds to the path through the dimensions outlined by Eames. It is the persistence of curiosity that will lead us to discover new semantic references in considering technical materials as defining the scope of the possible,[9] as a consequence of which we arrive at a canon of values for smart surfaces.

The new materials with their "alchemical properties"[10] allow new ways of thinking about elementary design questions, as formulated through the categories of

4
"Miniaturization is beneficial for enhancing mechanical stability, increasing mechanical resonance frequencies, increasing lifetime and increasing the efficiency of actuating forces in direct comparison to those forces causing material fatigue." See Hillmer et al. (2008), Sun Glasses for Buildings, p. 135.
5
Mazé (2007), Occupying Time, p. 35.
6
"Materials are no longer found. Rather, we can now engineer materials to achieve a specific, desired performance." Manzini (1996), The Material of Invention.
7
See Roland Barthes' remarks on sculpture. Barthes (1964), Mythen des Alltags [Mythologies], pp. 79–81.
8
In the words of Bruce Sterling: "Tomorrow composts today [...] new capacities are layered onto older ones" Sterling (2005), Shaping Things, p. 14.
9
See Finckh (2004), Oberflächen semantisch/funktional. Proceedings "Materialwechsel".
10
See Barthes (1964), Mythen des Alltags [Mythologies], p. 79.

nano, light, energy, climate and information. To a certain degree, they reflect parameters that have probably been surveyed most comprehensively, from a design viewpoint, in the *Massive Change* project initiated by Bruce Mau. Mau takes a very proactive stance when he relates design to a series of key concepts that are essentially intended to encompass all current global developments, in their present critical state.[11] Ultimately, it cannot be disputed that virtually all activities in the field of design and architecture[12] are determined at least indirectly by this large scale. Against this background, specifications of the locus of design form the second level on which to discuss the question of the intelligence of surfaces. A series of enlightening positions can be found on this aspect. John Thackara develops his ideas with reference to a series of comparatively abstract concepts, of which, interestingly, *lightness* forms the opening and *smartness* the actual conclusion. In a situation in which the most positive concepts imaginable have suffered through repeated appropriation, Thackara frees them from their ballast and points out the problems: "Man-made smartness tends to be overly complicated."[13] For Thackara, smartness stands, in a positive way, for a design that is oriented on the model of nature[14] and collective action oriented on ecological and social considerations.[15] *Lightness* in contrast, is an ideal. It implies the responsible use of resources and the idea, which is not essentially new, of appropriateness. Above all, however, *lightness* demands methodical openness and freedom from ideology.[16] The feeling conveyed in Thackara's argument that technology tends to lead to more complicated design, despite all good intentions, implies a wish to simplify things, a desire for reaction. Simplicity as an emanation of intelligence finds its expression in the formulation of simplicity as the art of the complex. John Maeda describes this art as a process of concealing the immediately understandable aspects while preserving the feeling for the inherent values. His formulation of simplicity as considered reduction is reminiscent of the classic formulations found in the field of architecture.[17] They are formulated more precisely through Paola Antonelli's arguments, according to which simplicity, as something non-stereotypical, is constituted not on a formal level, but on a structural level. Simplicity means knowing, with certainty, the purpose of something. It means that things *are* simple rather than simply appearing simple. The simpler they are, says Antonelli, the better their potential can come into play and be fully exploited.[18] Using an idiosyncratic terminology, science fiction author Bruce Sterling describes intelligence as an aspect of the subject-object relationship. He predicts

11
Urban Economies, Energy Economies, Information Economies, Image Economies etc. The project emphasises the imperative of design: "It's about the design of the world." See Mau et al. (2004), Massive Change.

12
The Design Dictionary ed. by Erlhoff and Marshall (2007) declines to give a precise definition, referring to the numerous sub-disciplines and specialisations. Where not differentiated more precisely, the terms 'design' and 'architecture' are generally used in their pragmatic sense in the following.

13
Thackara (2005), In the Bubble, p. 195.

14
Thackara focuses on the concept of biomimicry, not without reference to the related concepts of bionics, biomimetics, bioconstructivism etc. See Thackara (2005), p. 187.

15
"Smart Recombination of [...] edge people, edge ideas and edge organization [...] to foster innovations." See Thackara (2005), pp. 217–218.

16
With Italo Calvino, Thackara speaks of "different perspective, different logic [...] and fresh methods of cognition and verification". Thackara (2005), p. 27.

17
Maeda (2006), Law 1: Reduce, pp. 18–21.

18
Antonelli, Maeda (2006), The Goal of Safety is about as Simple as it Gets, pp. 28–29.

the transition from a technological present characterised by unstable, Baroquely multifunctional objects (*gizmos*)[19] to a world of unspecified, overwhelmingly rich, residue-free realisations of data-based, immaterial systems (*spimes*) in which design stands for a refined negotiation of technosocial relationships.[20] This culminates in a fusion of objects and subjects into surface entities (*biots*) based on the technical ideal of the synthetic skin CLIMATE Technical Background 3, p.127: "Living tissues have many industrial advantages: they grow at room temperature, they can use solar power, their products and effluents are mostly compostable, they scale rather easily, and, basically, we human beings get built that way ourselves."[21] Ramia Mazé's approach of weaving[22] refers at this point to the tradition, dating back to the handicrafts tradition, of producing surfaces in the form of fabric, which allows us to create envelopes for the body and for spaces. The aspects of surface intelligence manifested in dealing with fabrics range from clothing via the lightweight nature of nomadic tents up to the complex form-finding processes of membrane architectures. Weaving in-

volves the formation of space through nothing other than surface. **ill. Surfaces.16.1, p. 46.** A further-reaching interpretation of fabric is the idea of the congruence of both material-based and immaterial construction, of supporting structure and network INFORMATION Technical Background 2, p.144 which is expressed in the *Fiber Architecture*. **ill. Surfaces.03.1, p.44** Sterling's claim, derived from the problem of complexity, that not everyone can be a designer, is opposed by the principle of *Do It Yourself (D.I.Y.)*. Through the continuing process of simplification and miniaturisation of computer intelligence, D.I.Y. is developing, in a new way, into an important position within design.[23] INFORMATION Technical Background 3, p.155 Changes in production conditions promote both the individual and the participative, artistically experimental prototypical design of intelligent surfaces within the bandwidth of 'bricolage', improvisation of the temporary, as well as the professional, integrative solution.

A third general level of considering surface intelligence is represented by the clearly practice-oriented positions found in the sphere of architecture and building. The concept of lightweight construction

William Gibson, Neuromancer, Kap. 2

The air was damp and close with the smell of sweat and concrete. [...] No light but the holograms that shifted and flickered above the ring, reproducing the movements of the two men below.

[19]
In the words of Sterling, gizmos impose excessive cognitive burdens on us. The term refers to issues of artificial intelligence (AI). Research into AI is involved on two levels via information technology and cognitive science. See Gold (1998), Philosophical Aspects of Artificial Intelligence, p.50.
[20]
Sterling (2005), Shaping Things, p.22.
[21]
Sterling (2005), Shaping Things, p.136.
[22]
Mazé (2007), Occupying Time, p.71.
[23]
See Mazé (2007), Occupying Time, p.66. Kösch et al. (2008), Kluge Dinge.

represents a distinct approach to design in engineering science. Lightweight construction means using material resources efficiently in order to save material and thus energy. In lightweight construction one finds ideas for new envelopes, bodies and volumes that are constituted of surfaces, rather than manifesting themselves as mass. In the approach proposed here, lightweight construction represents the most consistent application of the concept of surface in terms of construction design. The engineer Werner Sobek defines lightweight construction as the school of understanding.[24] For him, the search for lightweight constructions involves searching for the limits, testing the boundaries of the physically and technically feasible, irrespective of the boundaries between disciplines. Lightweight construction also addresses the concept of the heavy (solid construction). Sobek makes a distinction between material lightweight construction, structural lightweight construction and system lightweight construction. Material lightweight construction refers to the use of building materials with a favourable ratio of specific weight to usable structural properties (strength, elasticity, rigidity). Here, new ultra-light material foams

(wood foam, metal foam, glass foam, nanogel), **ill. Nano.12.1, p. 26** Ultra High Pressure Concrete (UHPC) **ill. Surfaces.05.2, p. 57; Surfaces.05, p. 167,** sandwich materials **ill. Surfaces.14.1, p. 34** and composite materials **ill. Surfaces.15.1, p. 37; Surfaces.07, p. 173** extend the construction possibilities of intelligent surfaces. The aim of structural lightweight construction is the design of supporting structures of minimal weight. Structural lightweight construction represents the solution of a minimisation and optimisation problem within a design context hedged with restrictions. System lightweight construction refers to the principle by which, in addition to its load-bearing function, a building component also fulfils other functions, for example space-enclosing, storing, insulating or comparable functions. **ill. Surfaces.08.2, p. 12; Surfaces.08, p. 174** The load-bearing components thus become multifunctional, a solution which, in Sobek's view, is not consciously

Arthur C. Clarke, 2001 – A Space Odyssey, p. 43

The stewardess came walking up the narrow corridor to the right of the closely spaced seats. [...] She was keeping to the bright yellow band of Velcro carpeting that ran the full length of the floor —and of the ceiling. The carpet, and the soles of her sandals, were covered with myriads of tiny hooks, so that they clung together like burrs. This trick of walking in free-fall was immensely reassuring to disoriented passengers.

24
Sobek (2007), Entwerfen im Leichtbau [Designing lightweight structures].

made use of often enough in the building industry. Coatings, that is to say the boundary layers of materials in relation to the environment, deserve separate consideration. The protection of surfaces through the application of organic or inorganic coatings

is a particularly effective (and by no means obvious) strategy of material optimisation. Coating is an intelligent surface principle. **ill. Surfaces.06.2, p. 34;** NANO Technical Background 3, p. 75; **Surfaces.06, p. 171**

The way to designing intelligent surfaces leads from the boundary surfaces of the materials (exchange, absorption, trans-

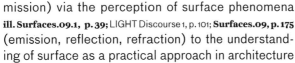

mission) via the perception of surface phenomena **ill. Surfaces.09.1, p. 39;** LIGHT Discourse 1, p. 101; **Surfaces.09, p. 175** (emission, reflection, refraction) to the understanding of surface as a practical approach in architecture and design, which demands a special readiness to compromise. Consistent surface design involves mediating the interactions of the technical with the artistic and of the ecological with the social, the results of which incidentally enrich humanity.

1 Inner space

Nanoscale refers to dimensions of the order of ten to the power of minus nine metres (10^{-9} m). The prefix 'nano' is derived from the Ancient Greek word for 'dwarf'. It is the decimal denotation for one billionth (one thousand-millionth) and indicates that the technical objects and structures being referred to are a certain number of nanometres, or billionths of a metre, in size.[1] The scientist and philosopher Alfred Nordmann has described this dimension, in which individual atoms and molecules can be differentiated, as nanospace. Nordmann views nanospace as a kind of 'inner space' (as opposed to 'outer space'), remarkable chiefly for the unlimited possibilities associated with this dimension.[2] The complex physical behaviour of objects changes beyond the microscopic scale at fewer than 100 nanometres. **fig. Nano scale, p. 76** Forces and effects that do not play a role at larger dimensions become significant below this threshold.[3] This may at first give the impression that the laws of nature operating in our macro world are ineffective at this scale. That is what makes the exploitation of nanospace so interesting: a macro world reaching its limitations gains access to new parallel worlds of physics, chemistry and biology.[4] The phenomena observed are directly attributable to the nanoscale dimension. This is why all relevant scientific definitions of nanoengineering[5] are now primarily based on the dimensional boundary. It is generally agreed that nanoengineering is concerned with the study, creation, application and manipulation of structures, molecular materials and systems that are between 1 and 100 nanometres in size. The 'inner space' metaphor implies that this area is broadly unexplored. At the same time, the word 'nanospace' expresses that we can move within this space, as well as design it. A lot of thought has been given to the nature of nanoengineering research. For the Harvard scientist Peter Galison, it marks a shift in emphasis.

1
Comparison: The relation between a large molecule with a diameter of one nanometre and a golf ball is similar to that between a golf ball and the Earth.

2
Nordmann (2007), Schöne, neue Nanowelt, p. 41.

3
Hillmer et al. (2008), Sunglasses for Buildings, p. 135.

4
A specialist in the philosophy of technology, Astrid Schwarz, has studied the background to Richard Feynman's pioneering lecture 'There's plenty of room at the bottom', which has fallen into obscurity. It was published in Engineering and Science, a journal of the California Institute of Technology, where Feynman lectured. Most of the articles and adverts in that issue were concerned with the imminent conquest of outer space, which it was hoped might offer solutions to overcrowding on planet Earth. In a climate of opinion marked by a 'hunger for space', as formulated by Schwarz (translated from the German), Feynman's vision formed a complementary advance towards a similarly empty 'inner space'. See Schwarz (2009), p. 10.

5
Henceforth, the term 'nanoengineering' will be used when referring to the area of nanoscience as a whole, while the term 'nanotechnology' will be used to denote a specific technology within that area. 'Nanotechnology' (in inverted commas) is in fact the official designation for the whole area, although this use is theoretically and linguistically incorrect.

Classically, acquisition of knowledge through research is based either on observation and reflection, or on assumption and experiment. The response of research to such observations is twofold: as ideas, i.e. through generating models and images that allow us to interpret and understand reality, and through the manifestations of the technology it produces. In nanoengineering, the fundamental sciences and the application-oriented strategies of the engineering sciences overlap. Galison calls this new practice *nanofacture*.[6] Nano research is always, according to Galison, an intervention that follows the dictum *making is knowing*. This characteristic may be interpreted as a paradigm shift, or as a distinct decrease in the reaction time between idea and action in the nanosciences, in the context of social realities. Alfred Nordmann, on the other hand, talks about *nanotechnoscience*, in which the role played by the acquisition, demonstration and communication of basic skills is still important. The first and foremost of these skills is visualisation: 'To start with, it has to be shown that objects in the nano world can in fact be seen, that objects can be moved and grown, and that it is possible to act there.' The symbolic founding of this nanotechnoscience came in 1989, when US scientists Don Eigler and Erhard Schweitzer used a scanning tunnelling microscope to 'write' IBM by manipulating 35 xenon atoms. According to Nordmann, this demonstrated the whole visionary potential of nanotechnology through: 'arbitrary technical control over individual atoms and molecules'.[7]

Stanislav Lem, Solaris, p. 98

At any moment, I should reach the limit of this exploration of the depths; the shadow of a molecule occupied the whole of the space; then the image became fuzzy. There was nothing to be seen. There should have been the ferment of a quivering cloud of atoms, but I saw nothing. A dazzling light filled the screen, which was flawlessly clear. I pushed the lever to its utmost.

2 Nano design

As such, the technical design of objects on a nanoscale is not as new as is often suggested. Nanoparticles were already being used in the Middle Ages: in processes such as staining window panes (gold nanoparticles in glass), or tempering swords (carbon nanoparticles in steel, as in the famous Damascus steel). An assessment of the current position of nano design necessitates making a number of assumptions. Many institutions with all sorts of backgrounds are involved in nanoengineering at a research level. Applications are generated by a huge number of individual research projects that generally have precisely defined objectives. As a rule, the majority of nanotechnology applications are developed for the technologically

6
Galison (2006), Nanofacture.
7
The story of nanotechnology has been told by many. See Jones (2007), Soft Machines. Steed et al. (2007), Core Concepts. Anderson et al. (2009), Nanotechnology—Risk and Communication.

advanced areas of aircraft and car manufacturing, machine construction and medical technology. Progressing from the development to the marketing stage, only a few applications, such as the nano-coated glass used for construction, can be said to belong clearly in the building industry. Knowledge transfer has allowed spatial design and the construction industries to benefit from many potential applications of nanoengineering. This situation leads to *technology-oriented concepts* of nano design being developed initially, usually encompassing nanoengineering process design and results. An understanding of the potential of a design can be gained from a systematic representation, such as that created by the British physicist Richard Jones. The advantage of Jones's model is that it explains applications in context with processes and the status of research in a manner that relates closely to architecture and design. Jones differentiates between 'incremental' and 'evolutionary' nanoengineering.[8]

3 Incremental nanotechnologies

The first 'incremental' nanoengineering category is also the most developed: this involves changing the structure of materials at nanoscale, giving rise to the name 'nanomaterial'. Among these are the so-called 'thin films': layers in which nanoparticles are arranged as regular nanostructured networks[9] deposited on carrier materials, or 'substrates'. When exposed to UV radiation, a process called photocatalysis allows these structures to break down films of dirt (composed of organic materials) into smaller

molecules, which can then be washed away, with the next rain for instance. ill. **Nano.10.1, p. 22; Nano.04, p. 166; fig. Photo-induced catalytic reaction, p. 79** Layers made of semiconductor nanoparticles or organic molecules capable of conducting electricity can, on the other hand, convert sunlight to electricity, allowing the production of extremely flat and flexible solar cells by rotary printing. ill. **Energy.08.4, p. 38;** ENERGY Technical Background 1, p. 89; **Energy.08, p. 176** Nanoparticles in suspensions (mixtures of liquid and solid components) are used in cosmetic or food products. The giant carbon molecules discovered about twenty years ago, known as 'fullerenes', are rather extraordinary. Cylindrical fullerenes are called 'nanotubes' and spherical ones are called 'buckyballs'. Their properties are of great interest to material science. As carriers of repair material, for

example, they play a role in the design of self-healing materials. ill. **Nano.06.1, p. 13** The addition of nanotubes can make plastics harder, electrically-conducting, or light-emitting. ill. **Light.16.1, p. 44;** ENERGY Technical Background 1, p. 89; LIGHT Technical Background 4.2, p. 113 Nanoparticles are also used as additives in high-strength concretes.

8
Jones (2007), Soft Machines, p. 7.
9
The smaller the particles of a material become, the greater is their total surface area (for the same quantity of matter). Therefore the structure of a material composed of nanoparticles is predominantly determined by boundary layers, a fact generally considered to be the cause of the highly reactive behaviour of source materials that are otherwise inert, and a fundamental characteristic of the new class of nanomaterials. See Nordmann (2006), Herbert Gleiter, pp. 84 – 85.

Incremental nanoscalability is, moreover, effective in highly efficient insulating materials, such as aerogel and in temperature-

regulating phase-change materials. **ill. Climate.11.1, p.14;** CLIMATE Technical Background 2.1, p. 122

The design potential of the currently usable incremental nanomaterials should be considered discriminately. Nanoengineering is often referred to as an enabling technology that intervenes in the material creation process at an early stage, quasi contained in semi-finished products as a value-adding feature. Most of the highly effective surface applications are in fact invisible. Thin nano films could theoretically also be coloured, but such decorative layers have not played a significant part in the market so far. The appearance of the materials used remains virtually uninfluenced by the film. Compared to the expected properties of the materials treated, the surface behaviour of the functional layers is manifested as an amazing effect, demanding to be observed like a physical experiment. Developers often use this manner of presentation, as a kind of ready-to-use application. The way things are at present, a 'nano house' is hardly any different from a conventional house, which is quite surprising in view of all the things that nanoengineering is thought to be capable of. **ill. Nano.10.2, p. 22; Nano.04, p. 166** Although its potential is being made use of, it has not yet had any considerable influence on the appearance, or design, of objects and structural components, apart from a few promotionally effective presentations and with the exception of the ultra-high-performance concretes (UHPC) under development. Contrary to the old dictum that new technologies bring about new morphologies, the diversity of potential applications in conjunction with characteristic visual unobtrusiveness may be considered to be advantages of the new technologies. These unusual features are nevertheless not entirely unproblematic, making the evaluation of a fundamentally new technology more difficult.[10] The system 'house' may be a good model to use at this stage (as opposed to the conceptual idea of 'skin' that evokes other design strategies), because it makes the new

Arthur C. Clarke, 2001 — A Space Odyssey, p. 10

It was a rectangular slab, three times his height but narrow enough to span with his arms, and it was made of some completely transparent material; indeed, it was not easy to see except when the rising sun glinted on its edges. [...] It was certainly rather attractive, and though he was wisely cautious of most new things, he did not hesitate for long before sidling up to it. As nothing happened, he put out his hand, and felt a cold, hard surface.

10
For an assessment of the consequences of the technology see Boeing (2006), Offene Nanotechnik. Anderson et al. (2009), Nanotechnology – Risk and Communication. For connections between new technologies, invisibility and design see Könches and Weibel (2005), unSICHTBARes.

possibilities of nanoengineering easier to understand. There are also some weaknesses, however, since the components constituting the system are only optimised in terms of process engineering: roofing tiles that look like ordinary roofing tiles; walls, windows, lamps; all sorts of known materials and surfaces are impressively better, more durable and more efficient than ever before. An important next step in exploiting the full potential of nanomaterials is to focus on technical functionality and sensory tactile aspects in design, rather than visual effect. INFORMATION Discourse 3, p. 135 Revised design specifications for high-strength materials such as UHPC, allowing the pro-

duction of slimmer and finer components, should open up new possibilities in solid and light-weight construction. **ill. Surfaces.05.2, p. 57; Surfaces.05, p. 167; fig. UHPC, p. 82**

4 Evolutionary nanotechnologies

The second category is referred to as 'evolutionary' nanoengineering by Jones: special public attention is devoted to suggestions that familiar technical principles such as machines or transistors operating on the basis of moving parts can be reduced to nanoscale.[11] These should, however, be considered critically. The status of the results obtained in this area of evolutionary nanoengineering is little more than hypothetical. The fact is that the precise, arbitrarily reproducible integration of different components to form more complex 'nanosystems' presents difficulties that are often only mentioned incidentally in official presentations. One of these is that prototypes are assembled in the lab using scanning electron microscopes—the second-most important nano tool invented in the 1980s—using processes that are so time-consuming that scaling them up to industrial scale is unlikely to be possible in the near future. Another is that the physical forces acting at a nano level, as mentioned earlier, stand in the way of applying macromechanical principles. Currently, the only available option seems to be component self-organisation. By modifying basic conditions such as working temperature, pressure or energy supply, nano researchers are trying to design self-assembly processes in a such way as to achieve more complex configurations of atoms and

molecules. Nordmann, however, points out that the nanocosmos is much more chaotic than is suggested by the paradigm of precise control of material. **ill. Nano.15.1,**

p. 54; ill. Information.27.1, p. 42 The thermal motion of atoms, the statistical behaviour of large ensembles of atoms in chemical reactions, and defects in atomic crystal lattices make an exact 'programming' of material, beyond the principle of self-organisation, almost impossible.[12]

11
Attention is drawn in this respect to the much-discussed concept of nanorobots, or nanomachines produced by means of molecular assemblers, formulated by K Eric Drexler. See Drexler (1986), Engines of Creation. Drexler's influence is reflected in the title of the American nanotechnology programme of 2000, 'Shaping Atom by Atom'. Jones's assumptions concerning soft machines are the counterparts of the 'hard' nanorobots. See Jones (2007), Soft Machines.

12
Recent research into the repulsive Casimir effect, however, give renewed impetus to speculation that nano-machines could be run without blockages. See Lindinger (2008), Casimir-Effekt. Also: Munday et al. (2008), Casimir-Lifshitz Forces, p. 170.

For Nordmann, concepts such as the nanorobot, based on the requirements and development of such programming, stem from the technological thinking of a bygone machine age.[13]

Further design strategies at other levels are to be expected in association with evolutionary nanoengineering. With this term, Jones refers to his own *Soft Machine*, which outlines the concept of a biological synthetic nanotechnology. Jones basically distinguishes between 'hard' nanostructures, made of silicon and carbon, and machines made of 'soft' biological building materials (such as artificial liposomes), which, according to this thesis, function better in nanospace conditions because of their similarity to the nanomachines constructed by nature.[14] The division of specific examples into 'hard' and 'soft' applications permits some insights into the potential of evolutionary nanoengineering for design-related disciplines. The visionary, poetic project *Construction in Vivo* involving a microstructured, breathing building skin developed by the architect Neri Oxman in conjunction with the nanoengineer John Hart, **ill. Nano.03.3, p. 29; Nano.03, p. 163** interprets a process-engineering rule of nano design which says that nanoengineering requires microengineering in order to be effective in macrospace.[15] An inherently nanostructured macrosurface, the reactions of which are not mechanically actuated, but which functions quasi biologically, is to be generated by growing nanotubes under the control of microengineering-based lithographic coating, printing and etching steps. Oxman and Hart illustrate their idea using 'hard' nanoengineering, but what is impressive is the consistent, process stage-related *(in vivo)* configuration of a building *skin*. One step towards realising this vision is the 'Active Window', a prototype developed at the University of Kassel in Germany. This involves a light control system composed of mobile micromirror arrays, which integrates nanoscale structures in a macro-object (window) using the microengineering methods described above. **ill. Nano.01.2, p. 52; Nano.01, p. 160** Because these micromirrors, made of silicon, are hardly visible, they allow a paradoxical kind of daylight control. Although fully transparent, the Active Window provides protection against sun and glare, as well as permitting adequate natural interior illumination. It supplies 'light in spite of shade'. The Active Window stands for the large scale application of 'hard' evolutionary processes.

13
The possible complications have been considered by Neal Stephenson in his science fiction novel 'Diamond Age': he describes a neo-Victorian 21st-century class society pervaded by nanomachines, in which every citizen is under total surveillance via ubiquitous nanosensors.

14
"The only true example of a nanotechnology we have available to study is cell biology [...] The advantage of this approach is obvious [...] Nature [...] has the use of the remarkable optimisation tool that is evolution and has produced very powerful and efficient nanomachines. We now understand enough about biology to be able to separate out a cell's components and to some extent utilize them outside the context of a living cell [...] This approach is quick and the most likely way to achieve radical nanotechnology soon." To illustrate his ideas, Jones also discusses research by Nadrian Seeman in New York, aimed at exploiting the recombination of DNA molecules for the targeted generation of spatial structures. See Jones (2007), Soft Machines, p. 125 and pp. 213 – 214.

15
On the systems engineering potential of micro-nano integration see. Botthof and Pelka (2003), Microsystems engineering.

₁ Basic principles of nanotechnological applications
Nanoengineering gives rise to an almost inestimable number of applications. Familiarisation efforts frequently culminate in a study of endless lists of applications and products that are ready for the market, imminently realisable or visionary, as popularly presented in public lectures or brochures. Attempts at systematisation are applicable only for a brief time, owing to the dynamic nature of this field of research. The nanotechnological applications currently relevant for design and the building industry can be differentiated in a variety of ways, for instance:

- Process engineering (PVD, CVD, sputtering, sol-gel processes, milling processes, special processes)
- Application (thin film, particles or coating, additive, composite, aerosol, colloid, dispersion)
- Function (protection, generation of light and energy, material optimisation, decoration etc)
- Context (fields of use).

Valuable insights can be gained from the different aspects considered by each of these systems of categorisation. For the sake of simplification, the category of 'incremental' nanoengineering NANO Discourse 3, p. 70 can be differentiated into *film and particle-forming processes*, from which the application areas *functional film and material optimisation* can be derived. These can be discussed with reference to context. NANO Discourse 2, p. 69 A corresponding subdivision for 'evolutionary' nanoengineering is of limited use, since all future and experimental developments are inherent in the term itself. Concepts such as the physicist Richard Jones's nano-based, synthetic, biological 'Soft Machines' and the attempts to come closer to the theoretically established (but technically challenging) 'Shaping Atom by Atom' have been discussed earlier. NANO Discourse 3, p. 70 Examples illustrating the possible applications of 'hard' nanotubes are presented at the end of this section.

2 Process engineering

The process engineering level is an important starting point for a dialogue between design and technical development, because this is where nano design starts. Problems relating to component size and geometry, for instance, which are similarly encountered in well-known processes such as galvanising or varnish coating, should however be considered individually. In terms of process engineering, almost all applications are generally based on the generation of films or particles. Methods for nanostructuring materials are popularly classified as 'top-down' or 'bottom-up'. Both groups are suitable for generating films and particles. The top-down principle involves breaking material down mechanically or chemically from larger to smaller structures, all the way to nanoscale. Particle sizes of 3–25 nm can, for example, be achieved with the industrially widespread method of using ball mills to reduce the size of mineral components. The bottom-up method is based on fabricating nanosized particles from the smallest available basic units of matter, i.e. atoms or molecules. The very successful sol-gel process (also known as chemical solution deposition) uses mixtures of two components that react with each other in droplet-shaped reaction volumes of a carrier substance to form nanosized particles. Another method of generating nanostructured surfaces is by the deposition of thin films on a substrate.

3 Thin films

The thin film process is a basic method for optimisation and new development of material that is predestined for use in the building industry and in design. The materials developed in this way are classified as 'new materials' and offer exceptional material and functional properties for solving the specific types of problem faced by various user groups. They could play an essential role in determining the future of many areas of building. Thin films increase the utility value of materials by modifying the surface properties. In practice, virtually all basic materials, such as glass, steel, aluminium, plastic, brass, various textiles and ceramic materials, can now be coated with thin films or film systems as required. Common coating materials include oxides, ceramics, inorganic materials, and metals, notably silver, gold, titanium oxide or carbon.

The typical thickness of a single layer in thin film processes ranges from one nanometre to ten micrometres fig. Nano scale, p. 76, which is well below those achieved by galvanising or varnish coating. The scope of application is extensive, pervading even our daily lives. Almost every product in modern information and communication technology relies on the special physical properties of thin films. These ubiquitous items could not be manufactured without vacuum deposition processes. Vacuum and plasma processes are used to deposit thin nanotechnological films on materials referred to as substrates. A special feature of the processes and applications is that they allow advance specification of a catalogue of requirements to solve given

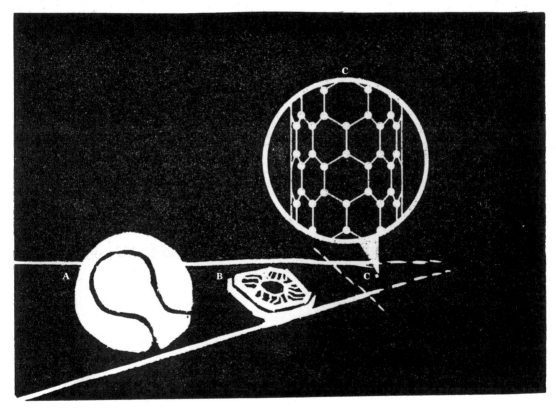

fig. Nano scale
A = macro, B = micro, C = nano, 100 nm = dimensional boundary, nano

problems, using standardised equipment systems. The functional layers obtained alter the material properties of the substrate significantly. In general terms, the application of a thin film involves the vapour deposition of pure metals, or alloys, on substrates in a vacuum environment. New and further-developed coating techniques in the

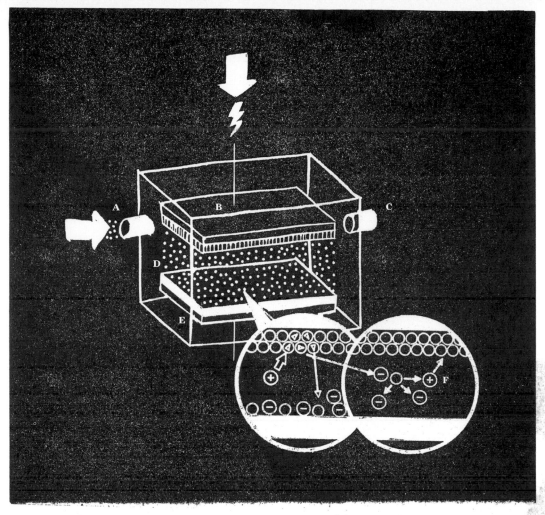

fig. Sputtering
A = argon reaction gas, B = cathode & target, C = evacuation valve, D = plasma, E = anode & substrate,
F = ongoing reaction at cathode/target

field of thermal vaporisation, such as pulsed magnetron sputtering (PMS) and plasma-activated high-rate evaporation (physical vapour deposition, PVD fig. Sputtering, p. 77), or the CVD (chemical vapour deposition) process, can be used to change specific functional properties of a whole range of basic materials. In contrast to wet-chemical processes, in which water-based or solvent-containing coating materials are deposited (preferentially by the sol-gel process) on a substrate as a single layer, the methods mentioned above generally allow the flexible combination of a number of layers. A great number of materials with adjustable film properties are available for deposition by the various processes. These can be applied, in turn, to a broad range of substrates. Conventional coating, finishing, pre- and after-treatment can furthermore be combined with these methods. On account of this systematic determinability, these new functional layers have opened up possibilities for the targeted optimisation of materials and components, as illustrated by the following examples.

3.1 Appearance—Decorative applications

The appearance of thin film-coated surfaces is partly determined by the substrate. In addition to various metallic surfaces, the colours achievable range from golden (titanium nitride, TiN; zirconium nitride, ZrN), reddish and bluish (titanium aluminium nitride, TiAlN; zirconium aluminium nitride, ZrAlN) to grey-blue and anthracite (titanium carbonitride, TiCN). The films may, however, also exhibit colour interference, or be transparent. Thin films reproduce the structure of the substrate. The appearance of a highly polished, micro-blasted, brushed or otherwise structured surface is retained after vacuum deposition, permitting its utilisation as an intentional design element. Such bond and interference coatings for decorative applications are used in fittings, articles of daily use and exterior cladding. They can be combined with functional protective coatings, such as those for enhancing scratch and corrosion-resistance.[1]

3.2 Photocatalytic and photohydrophilic coatings

Semi-conducting titanium dioxide layers (TiO_2) deposited by sputtering or high-rate electron beam evaporation on metals, glass or plastics are highly interesting as functional layers, owing to their photocatalytic and photohydrophilic properties. Photocatalysis refers to the activation of chemical oxidative or reductive processes in the coating by UVA light or sunlight, giving rise to the degradation of organic and inorganic substances lying on the surface. The hydrophilic properties of the coating lead to the contact angle of the water on the film surface being reduced to less than 110°. The consequently reduced flow resistance assists in forming a thin film of water and dislodging the degraded substances. On account of the semiconducting nature of the compound, titanium dioxide coatings have an antistatic effect, which results in the particle-repellent action displayed by plastic components, or varnished surfaces.

 These socalled non-stick or self-cleaning effects (easy-to-clean, lotus effect), ill. Nano.10.1, p.22 anti-fog

[1] Siegert (2004), PVD coating as design element. Proceedings "Materialwechsel".

effects, self-disinfecting and odour-killing properties can be taken advantage of in interior finishing work, the design of façade systems and other exterior applications. **ill. Nano.10.2, p.22; Nano.04, p.166; fig. Photo-induced catalytic reaction, p.79**

3.3 Scratch and corrosion-protection coatings

Organically modified coatings made of silicon oxide layers are particularly resistant to wear and abrasion. These hard and transparent coatings are ideal for stainless steel parts, providing effective protection from scratching and corrosion, coupled with a surprising anti-fingerprint action. They can also improve the long-term robustness of the surface of plastic parts.

fig. Photo-induced catalytic reaction
A = titanium dioxide TiO2, B = active oxygen CO3, C = NOx, D = NO3

Functional layers based on the reaction of titanium and nitrogen in the vaporisation process (titanium nitride, titanium aluminium nitride) are also characterised by an extraordinarily high resistance to abrasion and scratching, as well as very high corrosion resistance.

 ill. Nano.04.1, p. 13; Nano.04, p. 166 At the same time, the coatings produce easy-care surfaces. The degree of hardness of metallic surfaces such as steel or aluminium can be increased by factors between five and thirty-five in this manner.[2]

3.4 High reflectivity and absorption coatings

In order to improve the reflectivity of lighting or daylight control systems LIGHT Technical Background 2, p. 107, reflectors can be coated with silicon dioxide (SiO2) in combination with titanium dioxide (TiO2) by means of vapour deposition in a vacuum environment (PVD). The greater the difference in the refractive indices of the interference layers (SiO2—low substrate refractive index, TiO2—high refractive index),

the greater is the reflectivity of the reflecting surface. This physical effect produces an increase in lamp efficiency of approximately 10–20 percent. The reflectivity of specularly and diffusely reflecting surfaces can be increased by up to 95 percent.[3] ill. Nano.14.1, p. 31, ill. Light.14.2, p. 32 In a corresponding manner, losses due to reflected sunlight can be reduced by SiO2 anti-reflection coatings on glazing covering solar modules, thus increasing module efficiency by up to 5 percent.

ill. Nano.10.3, p. 22; ENERGY Technical Background 1, p. 89

3.5 Sun protection and thermal protection coatings

Thin films can be used to produce functional glass materials such as highly selective, low-emissivity (low-E) glass, sun-protection glass and transparent sun protection. In combination with the functional coatings already mentioned (easy-to-clean, lotus, anti-fog effect, antibacterial or microbicidal effects), this should enable highly specific solutions to be produced for particular problems. Coatings with thermotrophic properties, which react to temperature changes above a specific limit, are used in adaptive, controllable glazing systems with considerable potential for development. The scattering of light rays as they strike the glass can be varied in this application. Instead of being colourless and transparent, the

2
Metzner (2004), Transparent and coloured scratch-protection coatings. Proceedings "Materialwechsel".
3
Küster (2004), Surfaces for Daylight and Artificial Light. Proceedings "Materialwechsel".

glass reflects scattered white light, seeming opaque. In contrast, the control of glazing systems equipped with an ionised (i.e. slightly conductive) coating is independent of solar radiation. When a voltage is applied, this type of glass assumes a bluish colour, owing to the gas- or electro-chromatic effects of the coating. The glass can therefore be changed into highly effective solar protection at the flick of a switch. The degree of light transmission (and the total energy transmission) can be reduced by about 40 percent in this way.[4] ill. Surfaces.08.2, p. 12; Surfaces.08, p. 174

4 Methods for synthesising nanoparticles and carbon nanotubes
An important area of nanotechnological research concerns different ways of producing and using three-dimensional nanosized structures.[5] Since their discovery by the Japanese researcher Sumio Iijima in 1991, particles such as fullerene nanotubes (commonly referred to as carbon nanotubes or CNTs) and buckyballs (both named after Richard Buckminster Fuller because of their resemblance to the geodesic domes that he popularised CLIMATE Technical Background 1, p. 120) have attracted a lot of attention. These fascinating structures promise an enormous potential for development. CNTs are nanosized tubular structures (molecular nanotubes), the walls of which have a typical fullerene hexagonal honeycomb structure of carbon atoms. The tube diameter ranges from 1–50 nm, while the smallest tube produced has a diameter of only 0.4 nm. Single tubes may be several millimetres long, while tube bundles of up to 20 cm in length have been obtained. Nanotubes are categorised as single-walled (SWNTs) or multi-walled nanotubes (MWNTs), open or closed tubes, and empty or filled tubes (filled, for instance, with silver, liquid lead or noble gases). CNTs can be fabricated as a quantity of non-aligned material, or grown directly on substrates, the aim in the latter case being the production of aligned CNTs. ill. Nano.13.1, p. 28 The three most common production methods allow the control of diameter, wall structure (single-walled or double-walled) and deviations in the regular structure (defects). The ability to control length is, however, limited at present. All these parameters codetermine the properties of the material. Although CNTs are supplied by manufacturers on a gramme scale, batches are subject to a degree of tolerance and variation in the specification of the desired parameters.

4
Herlitze (2004), Modern Low-E Glazing. Proceedings "Materialwechsel".

5
The illustration fails to show the mechanical milling and sol-gel processes described earlier, with which particles and powder can likewise be manufactured.

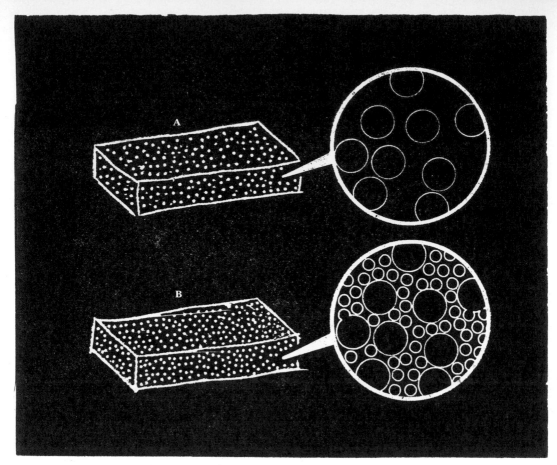

fig. UHPC
A = normal concrete, B = UHPC concrete with nano aggregate admixture

Three chief methods of synthesis with different variants have become established. Whereas the arc discharge method produces MWNTs quasi as a reaction and degradation product of two carbon electrodes, the laser ablation process vaporises graphite using a laser. The laser method is used for fabricating SWNTs. Nanotubes can also be synthesised by the catalytic decomposition of hydrocarbons; whole arrays of extensively parallel tubes can be grown on a substrate using the method of CVD (chemical vapour deposition). The process is often conducted with plasma-enhancement (PECVD). CVD is generally combined with photo-lithographic (microengineering) process steps. ill. Nano.01.2, p. 52 ill. Nano.03.2, p. 28; Nano.01, p. 160, Nano.03, p. 163 Photolithography transfers structural information from a photomask to a light-sensitive chemical (photo-resist) on the substrate. After exposure and development of the latent image, the structural information can be transferred to a layer underneath. The photoresist is removed afterwards. The procedure can be used to transfer complex and even relief-type structural information.

5 Applications of nanoparticles and carbon nanotubes

Applications of nanoparticles and carbon nanotubes are outstanding in the sense that they display a great number of special properties. In addition to their extreme mechanical strength, the electronic properties of CNTs, which can be either metallic or semiconducting, are particularly fascinating. High thermal conductivity and good chemical resistance are further qualities. These features and properties predestine these materials for sensory and actuatory applications, ill. Energy.21.1, p. 42, ill. Energy.22.1, p. 45; INFORMATION Technical Background 2.1, p. 146; fig. Sensor-Actuator, p. 150 as well as for use as field emitters, semiconducting components and energy storage devices. Although examples of the large-scale application of CNTs can already be cited (for example, as an additive for increasing the strength of plastics, such as those used to manufacture tennis rackets), their potential is probably nowhere near exhausted. As demonstrated by the previously mentioned *Construction in Vivo* project ill. Nano.03.3, p. 29; NANO Discourse 4, p. 72; Nano.03, p. 163 and the Active Window, ill. Nano.01.2, p. 52; Nano.01, p. 160 the possible creative applications of CNT or nanosized silicon structures are only just being realised. The great diversity of new developments to be expected is indicated by the following examples. In one case, researchers at the Rensselaer Polytechnic Institute, in New York, managed to create the darkest known synthetic material by the controlled growth of nanotubes.[6] ill. Nano.11.1, p. 23 Compared to conventional black paint, which reflects 5–10 percent of incoming light, the new material reflects only 0.16–0.18 percent. This effect is attributable to vertical nanotubes, which absorb a high proportion of incident light owing to their special alignment and to their surface structure, which can be described as having nanosized holes. It should be possible to increase the efficiency of solar systems significantly by exploiting these properties. ENERGY Discourse 2, p. 86 The aligned growth of CNTs allows highly adhesive

6
See Lin (2008), Darkest man-made material.

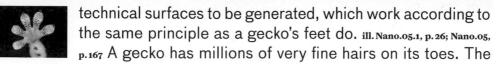 technical surfaces to be generated, which work according to the same principle as a gecko's feet do. ill. Nano.05.1, p. 26; Nano.05, p.167 A gecko has millions of very fine hairs on its toes. The contact surface area provided by these hairs is so large that enormously effective forces of attraction act between the hairs on the feet and the molecules of the substrate. These are the van der Waals forces, which under normal circumstances are hardly measurable. The total adhesive power of four gecko feet could hold about 140 kg. Researchers at the Georgia Institute of Technology have created a structure consisting of arrays of vertically aligned and horizontally coiled nanotubes, which has extraordinary adhesive capability; this is attributed to the arrangement and the electrostatic properties of the CNTs. The adhesive strength of a strip of prototype Gecko Glue tape of 3 × 3 cm is enough to hold up to 100 kg. The dry adhesive sticks to various rough and smooth surfaces (glass, plastic) and can be used reversibly. The tape could be used instead of magnets, or for equipping robots able to climb vertical surfaces, or for high-strength, flexible connections between building structures and façade components in mobile constructions.[7]

The term 'nanopaper' encompasses a number of developments by different research groups. These generally involve an easy-to-use, familiarly minimalist material with extraordinary properties. The paper developed from renewable nanosized cellulose fibres is as tearproof and elastic as the high-strength plastic material Kevlar. Electrostatic properties are optimised by adding small quantities of nanotube material. Nanopaper therefore represents an extremely strong, foldable and cuttable material that could be used to build objects, rooms and electronic components, and which is additionally able to store energy like a battery.[8] ill. Nano.07.1, p.19

7
Wang, Dai et al. (2008), Carbon Nanotube Arrays with Strong Shear Binding-On.
8
Henriksson et al. (2008), Cellulose Nanopaper Structures. Pushparaj et al. (2007), Flexible energy storage devices based on nanocomposite paper.

1 Designing energy-generating surfaces

'Energy harvesting'[1] ENERGY Technical Background 1, p. 89 encompasses many areas of scientific research advancing the interdisciplinary development of systems for tapping omnipresent energy potentials, in addition to the familiar methods of generating renewable energy. In the near future, n ew types of solar cell, piezoelectric ceramics, thermoelectric generator and biofuel cell will allow mechanical, thermal or organic energy to be converted to electric current everywhere. Energy is all around us, whether in the

form of solar radiation, wind or mechanical forces. ill. Energy.07.1, p. 48, ill. Energy.16.1, p. 31; Energy.07, p.175 The energy flow from the sun that reaches the earth's surface during one hour corresponds to the energy consumption of the whole world in one year. Mankind has always tried to find ways of making use of

this energy. While this has involved using complex constructions and techniques on one hand, very simple methods have often sufficed on the other, for example the harnessing of water power generated by natural gradients in the flow of the water. A turning point came in the USA in 1954, with the development of the first functioning solar cells using the semiconductor material silicon. From then on, it was established as fact that energy can be created and transformed within a surface of just a few millimetres in thickness. The efficiency of this technology[2] over a longer period of time, in an environment that is completely hostile to life, was clearly demonstrated by Vanguard 1, the first satellite equipped with such modules, which was sent into space in 1958. This first generation of solar modules heralded a completely new era in energy generation: the silicon solar cell is considered the material embodiment of a complete change in the supply of energy, allowing local generation of an unlimited quantity of electricity, completely without emissions and noise. Based on the example of energy self-sufficient satellites able to operate for decades in outer space, the 'micro power station' concept applied

1
The term 'energy harvesting' describes the 'harvesting' of energy found in the immediate surroundings (oscillations, temperature, flow, light) and the conversion of this energy to electricity. 'Energy harvesters' are generally autonomous transformers such as thermo generators, solar cells, or piezoelectric elements. Although the expected energy yields are generally low, longer operating times can be achieved for self-sufficient systems by appropriate dimensioning and system optimisation. See Priya and Inman (2009), Energy Harvesting Technologies, pp.3-7.
2
See Markvart and Bogus (2000), Solar electricity, p.3.

to our homes is intended to guarantee the continuation of our modern standard of living, even in times troubled by worries about energy scarcity and subsequent price increases. Contemporary discussions about the properties of energy-generating surfaces usually presume confidence in the technical capacity of such systems.

2 Power station versus building

Although many reasons for a different approach may exist, the methods of energy generation used are chiefly determined by economic aspects. The superficially attractive 'power station metaphor' being the basis of all concepts, buildings are consequently seen as power stations, with their skins following suit. This logic, however, measures success on the basis of capital efficiency, which is derived from the relation between the investment costs, service life and efficiency of a system. This actually forces the majority of alternative approaches to energy generation to follow the old rules of large-scale technical systems. As far as energy-generating surfaces are concerned, the silicon solar cell continues to remain the 'work horse' that researchers and manufacturers alike are eagerly trying to optimise with regard to its cost-benefit efficiency. This is evident in the number of photovoltaic efficiency records reported at regular intervals. A specific design of energy-generating surfaces will, however, be very difficult to develop in this manner. Although the technical parameters of energy-generating surfaces can be varied theoretically—as far as conventional solar cells are concerned this involves the angle of inclination of the modules, as well as their internal structure, colour, material and format—the scope of interpretation is severely restricted by the power station dictum. Any deviation in design resulting in even the slightest reduction in efficiency cannot be implemented from an economic point of view. In their efforts to utilise solar energy, engineers and architects have entered a field called *Building Integrated Photovoltaics (BIPV)*, where they are trying to get away from seeing energy-generating surfaces only as a kind of application and are allocating additional building skin functions to the surfaces instead. Photovoltaic

Stanislaw Lem, Solaris, p. 98

Beneath my gaze, sharply foreshortened, was a vast desert flooded with silvery light, and strewn with rounded boulders [...] which trembled and wriggled behind a veil of mist. [...] The crater, bristling with silver ion deposits, extended beyond the microscope's field of vision. The nebulous outlines of threads of albumen, distorted and atrophied, appeared in the midst of an opalescent liquid. A worm of albumen twisted and turned beneath the crosshairs of the lens. Gradually I increased the enlargement.

elements can, for instance, replace the roof or façade skin, or provide solar protection in parallel. The driving force behind development in this area is solar thin film technology, which in   the meantime is able to accommodate 'micro power stations' in increasingly thin and flexible films. NANO Discourse 3, p. 70 These can, moreover, be applied to al- most any form of substrate, including glass, metal or plastic. ill. Energy.12.1, p. 16 The format, formability and colour design of the solar modules[3] are also flexible. ill. Energy.11.1, p. 16 As demonstrated by the example of the thin film solar cell, the design of energy-generating surfaces is not currently hampered by a lack of technical possibil- ities. Technological approaches providing a great number of dif- ferent design options that meet a wide range of modern require- ments and living contexts are already available for the design of photovoltaic, thermo- and piezoelectric 'micro power stations'. Designing usage scenarios first, prior to the realisation of ob- jects and rooms, could be a way for the new technolo- gies to establish themselves faster. ill. Energy.04.1, p. 18; Energy.04, p. 168 Instead of the exclusive one-dimension- ality of maximum energy yield and expensive (neces- sarily durable) systems,[4] better solutions could be provided in future by open-system, low-tech, low-budget applications (more prone to wear) or high-quality, intentionally 'material-oriented' designs in combination with usage relationships in which the power station function is, as it were, hidden as a bonus. De- sign would therefore not be limited to installing the right system of prefabricated components. This would open up opportuni- ties latent in considering energy-generating surfaces as semi- finished products. The sustainability of such strategies could be quantitatively expressed by the diversity of possible applications and the potential to open up market opportunities for forward- looking technologies. ill. Energy.08.4, p. 38; Energy.08, p. 176 Such a context-oriented energy design would be an open- ing alternative to defensive, building-integrated photo- voltaics. It could be based on a few general principles (decentral organisation, pursuit of new technical approaches, diversification, polymorphism). Although the design of en- ergy-generating surfaces has to continue to deal with the argument of economically measured effi- ciency, this could also lead to it being increasingly understood in the context of an interconnected system. In terms of energy engineering, i.e. with regard to energy production methods, this means building up a network of innumerable small and medium-sized collector areas that are integrated in the network of large power station units, now still running on fossil fuels. Despite their often small individual capacities, these are certainly efficient in combination.[5] Designers should not be awed by an

3
See Luque and Hegedus (2003), Handbook of Photovoltaic Science, pp. 1005–1041.
4
Most PV module manufacturers specify guarantee periods of 20 years and above. Although module per- formance decreases with age, manu- facturers normally also specify a minimum performance guarantee over the module service life. See EPIA (2007), Solar Generation 4, p. 17.

apparently complicated technology. An understanding of the basic interrelationships normally suffices for conducting 'material-appropriate' experiments and research. The objective is to find basically undogmatic design solutions, ideally leading to new developments that are equally functional and aesthetic. This would prevent sustainability being assessed primarily on the basis of energy figures and would allow better technologies based on intelligent design to establish themselves. INFORMATION
Discourse 3, p. 135

5
The aim of the concept of a 'virtual power station' is to produce more in line with consumer consumption (and thus avoid expensive national power consumption peaks) by combining many individual energy generation systems of various types and sizes. The systems are controlled via a 'brain'—normally a computer-based control centre—that switches the systems on and off as required.
See Schubert (2008), Ersatz für Regelenergiekraftwerke, pp. 30–35.

ENERGY Technical Background

[1] Sunlight-converting surfaces

A simple way of making use of solar radiation is to absorb solar heat. Even simply covering a swimming pool with a black plastic mat (solar mat[1]), which causes the water in the pool to heat up, illustrates this principle of solar thermal energy. However, the higher operating temperatures required for household hot water use cannot be achieved in this way. Working on the same principle as a greenhouse, in which the sun's rays and the reflected heat are prevented from escaping again, the effect is intensified if the absorber (in this case the mat) is enclosed inside an envelope. The captured thermal energy can be distributed and utilised by means of a system of pipe loops running through the absorber which contain a carrier medium (liquid or air). This strikingly simple climate-control principle, which covers the entire radiation spectrum, can be used in diverse ways, ranging from simple applications to concepts involving solar thermal energy systems integrated into buildings. Although *solar thermal energy* simply produces thermal flows, rather than generating electricity directly, this thermal flow can be used in a variety of ways for the consumer-oriented, emission-free climate control of buildings.[2] CLIMATE Technical Background 2.3, p.127 *Flat plate collectors* and *vacuum tube collectors* are alternatives generally used in solar thermal energy systems where higher outputs are required. In *flat plate collectors*, the heat

[1] The simplest form of the solar pool mat is black sheeting. More complex variants pass the pool water through a hose system contained in the absorber mat. See Quaschning (2008), Erneuerbare Energien und Klimaschutz, pp. 138–139.

[2] In its "Vision for Solar Thermal Energy" for the year 2030, the European Technology Platform for Solar Thermal Energy (ESTTP), founded in 2005, formulates the goal of increasing the possible contribution of solar heat to the overall demand of a building from 25–30 percent, as is usual today, to 100 percent for new buildings in the future ("active solar house"). Another goal is the implementation of technologies which make it possible to convert thermal energy into electricity or "solar cooling". Such systems for using collected solar heat to run refrigerating units have the advantage that the greatest cooling loads occur at the same time as high inputs of solar radiation. See http://esttp.org/cms/front_content.php.
The Worcester Polytechnic Institute (WPI) is investigating the possibility of transforming large areas of asphalt, such as car parks, into collector surfaces. The heat generated in this way could be used for the climate control of nearby office buildings. See www.wpi.edu/News/Releases/20089/asphaltnews.htm.

transfer medium is located within the *absorber*[3] NANO Technical Background 5, p.83 contained in a flat, heat-insulated casing covered by a glass plate. Transmission of sunlight ensures that the carrier medium within the absorber is warmed up. Subsequent heat losses through convection are

 reduced by insulation. However, these can only be prevented completely by running the carrier medium within a vacuum, as is the case for vacuum tube collectors. Although the operation of this system is extremely efficient, the vacuum represents a source of manufacturing faults and problems. **ill. Energy.23.1, p. 47**

The direct conversion of sunlight to electricity, an area referred to as *photovoltaics*, operates according to a principle that has been known for a very long time, the photoelectric effect.[4] For many years, *thick film solar cells* based on *crystalline silicon* were the standard. Even today, in industrial manufacturing they produce the highest efficiencies and are the most frequently installed system variants. *Thin film technology*, developed during the 1980s and currently increasing in importance NANO Technical Background 3, p.75 leads to completely different applications and to a different understanding of *building-integrated photovoltaics (BIPV)*, a branch that is benefiting from the development of solar cells from a "high tech, high budget" product into a "high tech, low budget" one and is challenging the applicability of the 'power plant' metaphor. ENERGY Discourse 2, p.86, INFORMATION Discourse 2, p.133 In this connection, it is useful to categorise solar cells into three generations:[5]

- First generation (crystalline silicon solar cells)—the aim here is above all to achieve high efficiencies in order to justify the high investment costs
- Second generation (thin film solar cells)—the aim is to reduce costs while accepting, at present, still slightly lower efficiencies
- Third generation (concentrator cells, nanostructures, organic and dye-

3
Absorbers are continually being developed further in order to improve their energy yield. Normally, a body that absorbs radiation well also radiates heat well. In order to minimise the associated energy loss, selective absorbers are almost always used. A special coating allows them to absorb radiation very efficiently within the range of short-wave solar radiation and at the same time emit very little long-wave thermal radiation. This significantly improves the efficiency of the collector.
See www.solarthermietechnologie.de/technologie/kollektoren/flachkollektoren.
Of interest in this connection is research conducted by the Rensselaer Institute which, with the aid of nanotechnology, has developed the world's blackest black. A carpet of minute nanotubes absorbs 99.95 percent of all light, which could make it an ideal absorber material. See Lin (2008), Darkest manmade material.
4
In 1839 Alexandre Edmond Becquerel discovered that electrons are liberated from a metal surface when this is hit by electromagnetic radiation.
5
Green (2003), Third generation photovoltaics, pp. 1–4.

sensitised cells, thermophotovoltaics)—new approaches in terms of technology and materials are aimed at enabling thin film solar cells to achieve higher efficiencies and at opening up new areas of application, while reducing manufacturing costs

The most efficient monocrystalline silicon solar cells of the first generation employ a layer structure in which all modern crystalline cell types have their origin, despite certain differences in detail: a conducting material *(rear contact)* is applied to a carrier material *(substrate)*, which is responsible for structural stability. This is followed by the actual light-converting *(photoactive)* layer, which absorbs photons and generates free electric charge carriers. These then reach another conducting material *(front contact)* at the top of the cell, thereby allowing a flow of current when any electricity-consuming device is connected. Groups of these individual solar cells are connected in series via contacts to form *solar modules*. fig. **Photovoltaic, p. 92** The substance most commonly used for converting light to electricity is still silicon. This is, however, attributable not so much to a particular superiority of the material, but rather the production process involved. Silicon is made by melting plain quartz sand. It established itself early on as the obvious material to use, because the parallel development of the semiconductor market was making it available in large quantities. Crystalline silicon solar cell production involves sawing 250 µm thick slices from silicon blocks. The silicon wafer thus obtained assumes two functions: it is the layer that generates charge carriers, as well as the substrate that gives the cell structural stability. The latter necessitates a greater quantity of material, however, which leads to high costs.[6] Nor do multicrystalline wafers, which are simpler to manufacture, make much of a difference in this respect. New technological approaches primarily aim to save on silicon in order to achieve higher energy yields with significantly less material input.

 Research in this area has led to completely new material concepts and techniques. ill. **Energy.17.1, p. 32**

6
Silicon is grey by nature. The typical bluish colour is added later in order to optimise the absorptive capacity of the cell for the light spectrum that it can use. It could also be coloured green, violet or brown, but most manufacturers do not go in for these alternatives because of the associated efficiency losses. See Quaschning (2008), Erneuerbare Energien und Klimaschutz, p. 109.

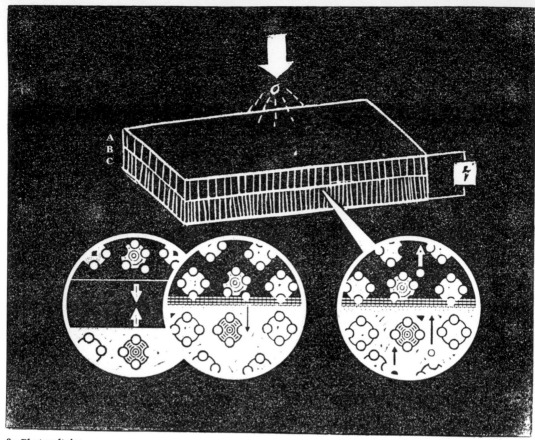

fig. Photovoltaic
A = n-doped silicon, B = boundary layer, C = p-doped silicon

The most advanced of these is the development of *thin film solar cells*, ill. Light.04.2, p.20; Light.04, p.168 in which the *photoactive layer* of silicon is kept as thin as possible. One variant involves the vapour deposition of amorphous silicon (a-Si). NANO Technical Background 3, p.75 This non-crystalline form is a direct semiconductor[7] and can therefore be applied in layers as thin as about 5nm. The most common substrate used is glass, but metal, ceramic, plastic (PVC) or thin films are also suitable. This makes the cell a lot less energy- and cost-intensive and also much more flexible as far as applications are concerned. The semiconducting properties of a number of other materials are currently being studied and new forms

7
Crystalline silicon is an 'indirect semiconductor': it only absorbs light when the energy of a penetrating photon is larger than the band gap of the material. A successful transition requires that the thermally oscillating crystal lattice also changes the pulse of the electron. Since a simultaneous change in energy level and pulse is unlikely, a wafer with a minimum thickness of 0.3 mm is needed to absorb the sunlight completely. The valence electrons of 'direct semiconductors', on the other hand, do not need to change their momentum to absorb the energy from a photon, which is why these are effective in thinner layers. See Rindelhardt (2001), Photovolvoltaische Stromversorgung, pp. 98–99.

of module are being developed. These include, in particular, CIS (copper indium selenide) and CIGS (copper indium gallium selenide) thin film solar cells, as well as cadmium telluride (CdTe) cells, which are already in widespread use. These are based on material systems[8] characterised by a particularly high and specific light absorption capacity, which makes them able to convert a larger proportion of the solar spectrum to electricity, even if radiation is only diffuse. Although the efficiencies of crystalline solar cells are at present still superior, thin film technology is opening up new design options. ENERGY Discourse 2, p.86 Shape, colour and application surface will vary a great deal more in the future, because the *deposition* of the photoactive layer on the substrate is a technique that opens up the possibility of being able to create significantly larger areas of varying geometries. The new production methods also make it unnecessary to interconnect each individual cell of a module, as with crystalline cells, using a copper wire. The large semiconductor layers obtained by deposition are divided into smaller cells with *integrated* wiring by using laser technology. ill. Energy.24.1, p.47; NANO Technical Background 2, p.75 Most thin film solar modules are coloured black or brown. New semiconductor materials, however, are enabling colour variations: colour design based on the absorption behaviour of the photoactive layer gives rise to only minor efficiency losses. The third generation offers a number of promising technologies. Beside the approach of optimising the energy yield per surface area through *tandem cells* or *concentrator solar cells*, particularly interesting possibilities are opened up by *organic photovoltaics (OPV)*. This technology, which is of major significance for solar cell research, involves developing electrically conducting polymers (plastics with completely new properties) to production stage. The advantage of such photoactive polymer films is their ease of production: after dissolving the material in a solvent, this can be applied by dripping, flinging or pressing it on to a suitable substrate. A homogenous film of only 100 nm in thickness is obtained after evaporation of the solvent. The potential of organic solar cells is extremely interesting for designers for two main reasons: the low production costs and the possibility of depositing them on virtually any foil. ill. Energy.12.1, p.16

8 In addition to silicon, CIS and CdTe solar cells, research is being carried out into many other material combinations suitable for solar thin film technologies. However, due to their even higher process costs, thin film solar modules are still not significantly cheaper than crystalline modules. Solar cells coated with gallium arsenide (GaAs), which are primarily used in space technology, are particularly expensive and efficient. www.eti-brandenburg.de/energie-themen/solarenergie/photovoltaik/duennschicht-solarzellen.html.

Significantly higher efficiencies can be achieved with tandem solar cells. In this technology, several cells are arranged on top of one another. The semiconductor material of the top layer is, for example, optimised for high photon energies (short-wave, blue spectral components), while that of the bottom layer is optimised for longer-wavelength light (green or red). The cells in the different layers are connected in series, so the voltages add up.[9] In concentrator solar cells, the semiconductor area is reduced to a minimum by concentrating sunlight on a smaller surface area, which the light, however, strikes with a greater intensity. This is normally achieved by using lenses or mirrors. ill. Energy.15.2, p.31 However, special holographic films applied to glass can also 'bundle' incident light of specific wavelengths and direct it to a solar cell optimised for that particular wavelength range. Such films can, for example, be used in solar cells integrated in the reveal of a window frame.

Another innovation is the *electrochemical dye-sensitized solar cell (Graetzel cell)*. This uses dyes to convert incident radiation to chemical energy, similarly to how plants use chlorophyll. Various dyes are currently being studied as potential photoactive layers. Two obstacles on the way from laboratory scale to large-scale applications are the durable long-term sealing of the dye and the efficiencies achieved under real conditions of use. While semi-transparent thin film solar modules are already being produced,[10] dyes that are totally transparent and yet able to convert a specific part of the visible light spectrum to electricity are as yet only a vision of the future in the field of organic photovoltaics. They would make it possible to have completely transparent thin films that generate energy from light of wavelengths invisible to humans, while letting through the visible spectrum. Although certainly reaching a limit from an aesthetic point of view, such solutions will always remain compromise solutions, because light that is not absorbed is energy lost. ill. Energy.11.1, p.16, ill. Energy.11.2, p.16, ill. Energy.11.3, p.16, ill. Energy.20.1, p.39 Researchers at Idaho National Laboratory are currently trying to use *thermophotovoltaics* to develop

9
The use of tandem cells is particularly worthwhile where high electricity yield and compactness are of the essence, for example in space technology. www.eti-brandenburg.de/energiethemen/solarenergie/photovoltaik/wirkungsgradsteigerung.html.
10
The cells are arranged in the substrate (usually glass) at intervals to each other, so that light passes through it between the cells; the solar cell itself is not translucent. The effect is comparable to a greyscale raster. Transparency and performance are dependent on the raster width.

cells that generate electricity even after sunset.[11] Such cells convert the invisible thermal infrared radiation that the earth emits at night as a form of the solar energy received during the day. To achieve this, tiny loops of conducting material, called nanoantennae NANO Technical Background 5, p. 83 are attached to a plastic film. The nanoantennae can be made of a number of materials, including gold, manganese and copper, and have a diameter of only a few nanometers, which is only a fraction of the diameter of a human hair.

2 Thermal energy-converting surfaces
No other man-made object is further away from the sun than the space probe Voyager 1.[12] In order to harvest energy on a long-term basis without depending on solar radiation, the probe uses *thermoelectric generators (TEG)*. These can transform small temperature differences of about 5°C into electric current. TEGs make use of the Seebeck effect:[13] electrons become more mobile, i.e. richer in energy, under the influence of heat. The difference in thermal energy between the warm and cold end of the semiconductor results in an electron concentration gradient. Such thermoelectric generators have for example been used in gas cookers, heating systems and electric cooling boxes for about fifty years already. Although it has not been possible to increase TEG efficiencies significantly until now, developments in thin film technology ill. Energy.25.1, p. 59; fig. Thermoelectrics, p. 96 promise significant increases in efficiency coupled with smaller size; such units should also be suitable for use within large, flat building components (surfaces). This makes concepts such as *Crowd Farming* NANO Technical Background 3, p. 75 viable. Efficient thermoelectric generators need to possess low thermal conductivity and high electrical conductivity, even though these parameters are closely linked to each other. Thanks to thin film technology, it is possible to apply extremely thin layers of materials with different thermoelectric properties on top of each other. While hindering thermal transport, the interfaces created in this manner do not impair the flow of current. Since thermoelectric generators are capable of converting even relatively small

11
See Idaho National Laboratory (2008), Flexible nanoantenna arrays capture abundant solar energy.

12
On board Voyager 1, launched in 1977, RTGs (Radioisotope Thermoelectric Generators) are used to gain the required operating warmth from the decay of plutonium 238 radioisotopes on board.

13
In 1821, Thomas J. Seebeck observed how a compass needle was deflected in the vicinity of two conductors which were of different types, but connected, if the temperatures at the connection points were different. In doing so, he had converted thermal energy into electrical energy. See BMBF (2005), Mikrosystemtechnik-Kongress, p. 407.

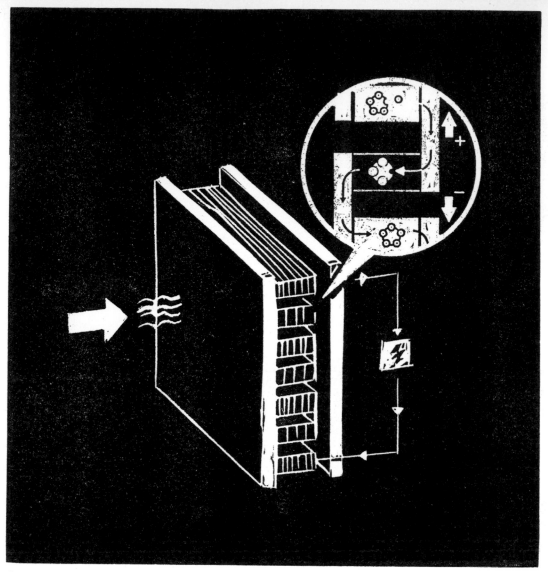

fig. Thermoelectrics

temperature differences into electrical energy, even differences of around 5°C, (between clothing and the surface of the skin, for example) are enough to supply a voltage of 5V/cm² .[14] This is sufficient for operating medical sensors, hearing aids or microelectronic chips in *Smart Clothing* applications. INFORMATION

Technical Background 3, p. 155

[14]
See Information sheet by Mikrosystemtechnik Baden-Württemberg e. V. (2007), Thermoelectric Energy Converters—Generating Electricity through Temperature Differences.

3 Pressure-converting surfaces

Piezoelectric elements, too, do not depend on solar radiation. The application of mechanical stress causes the centres of charge within a crystal to be displaced, resulting in a *dipole* and allowing electric current to be tapped.[15] ill. Energy.07.1, p. 48; ill. Energy.14.1, p. 26; Energy.07, p. 175; fig. Piezoelectricity, p. 98 In contrast to *piezoelectric crystals, piezoelectric ceramics* do not possess any natural piezoelectricity. They are, however, much easier to produce. The haphazardly arranged small polar regions left after sintering are aligned in a high voltage electric field (polarisation process). Typical starting materials are modified *lead zirconate titanate (PZT)* and *lead magnesium niobate (PMN)*. Piezoelectric ceramics are widespread nowadays: igniting the gas in ceramic lighters for instance; supplying actuators for wireless switching, or fulfilling a variety of sensor technology applications such as measuring vibration and pressure. INFORMATION Technical Background 2.1, p. 146 In future, rapid advances are particularly expected for research work involving *piezoelectric polymers (PEP)*.

Theoretically, all plastics can display an effect that is comparable to that of piezoelectric crystals without requiring any electrical pre-treatment at all. The decisive breakthrough in the field of *piezoelectric polymers* was achieved with a synthetic polymer, *polyvinylidene fluoride (PVDF)*. This flexible film has, in the meantime, made possible several pioneering applications. Piezoelectric loudspeakers, fast detec- tors and underwater sound transducers, for instance, already use PVDF. The piezoelectric dance floor also exists ill. Energy.06.1, p. 34; Energy.06, p. 173 and French scientists are busy trying to generate electricity from the impact of rain drops. Depending on the intensity of the rain, tiny currents are generated by a thin polyvinylidene fluoride surface.[16] An output of several thousandths of a watt has been achieved with test modules of only a few square centimetres in area. Only a small yield, perhaps, but enough to supply sensitive sensors with energy. Although the voltages generated by piezoelectric elements are very small, the interconnection of a number of elements makes it theoretically possible to create currents of any size. Each piezoelectric

15
An inverse application of the piezoelectric effect is also possible. A crystal will change its shape on exposure to an electric field. This is referred to as a reciprocal piezoelectric effect.

16
New Scientist (2008), Pitter-patter of raindrops could power devices. Jean-Jacques Chaillout's group at the French Atomic Energy Commission (CEA) in Grenoble.

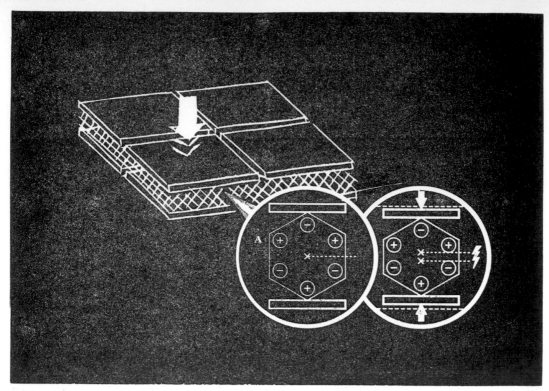

fig. Piezoelectricity
A = piezoelectric crystal

 element represents an independent micro power station that, combined as a virtual power station, could make objects and
buildings self-sufficient in energy. ill. Energy.01.2, p. 39; ENERGY Discourse 1,
p. 85; Energy.01, p. 164

₄ Conversion of sunlight using biomass surface reactors
A large quantity of the sunlight that falls on the Earth is converted to
biochemical energy by microorganisms. Whereas the electrical energy obtained from solar cells has either to be used directly or stored
expensively (one-stage conversion), microorganisms basically act
as a living store of solar energy (two-stage conversion).
ill. Energy.19.2, p. 36 The *microbial* or *biofuel cell* exploits this fact to
create electric energy from biomass. Such fuel cells depend
on bacteria to produce new decomposition products from
organic material, which in turn can be converted into electricity. Splitting sugar into small molecules is one way of doing this.
The principle is similar to the plant metabolism, in which light energy
is converted to chemical energy, accompanied by the creation of

oxygen and sugar (as reaction products), the latter being used as a kind of biocatalyst for transferring electrons. In the biofuel cell these free electrons are 'harvested' by an electrode. The resulting flow of current between the electrodes is sufficient to operate temperature sensors or measuring devices. fig. Biofuel, p. 99 In future, such fuel cells could supply mobile phones with energy, or use waste water in sewage treatment plants to generate electricity.

Although the excellent energy storage capacity of hydrogen makes this material very important, the synthesis of hydrogen is not yet adequately efficient. With their natural capacity to create hydrogen, microalgae are able to produce large amounts of energy continuously in closed pipe systems. Genetically modified microalgae

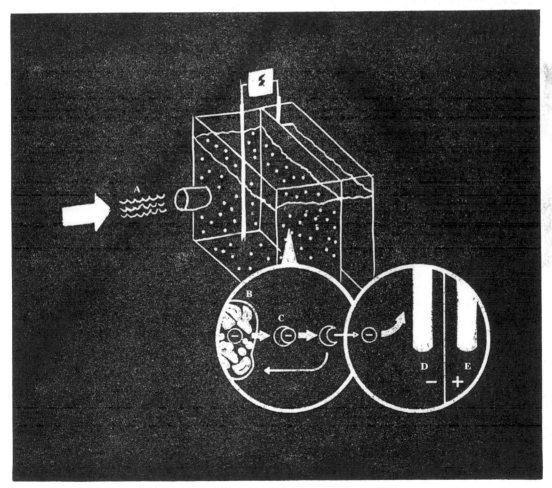

fig. Biofuel
A = wastewater-nutrient solution, B = algal organisms, C = transport particles, D = cathode, E = anode

can produce many times more hydrogen than their natural counterparts. Projects studying algae cultivation systems integrated in façade systems are in progress. While such building-integrated biomass surface reactors are still at the design stage, the large-scale cultivation of microalgae for operating biomass power stations has already passed the test phase.[17] ill. Energy.03.2, p. 55; ill. Energy.02.1, p. 47; ill. Energy.10.2, p. 12; Energy.03, p. 165; Energy.02, p. 164

17
The company Solix is planning a photobioreactor (PBR) which produces algae on an industrial scale, in order to process these into biodiesel. See www.solixfuels.com. For the basics of algal reactions, cf. Richmond, Amos (Ed.) (2004), Handbook of Microalgal Culture. Fitzwilly (2009), Make a Microbial Fuel Cell. Granel and Turner (2006), Ecology of Harmful Algae.

LIGHT Discourse

1 Optical spectacles versus optical technologies

At the interface of art and science, light has become of key importance as a medium in many areas. Although artificial light has always been a factor in the design and use of interior and exterior structures, today's optical technologies[1] LIGHT Technical Background 1, p.106 have made accessible previously undreamt of ways of using artificial and technical light. This applies to almost every area of science, including nanoelectronics. NANO Technical Background 4, p.81.

The incandescent lamp has long been surpassed by more innovative, energy-efficient and environmentally compatible sources of illumination.[2] The advantages offered by these new developments, such as continuously variable adjustment of the intensity of illumination and its colour, allow light to be used to create spectacular effects, motivating designers and planners to use lighting equipment in a more generous manner that consumes more energy. The emotional and associative potential of spectacular lighting installations as a communicative medium is often underestimated, with the visual spectacle generally dominating the intended message.

Light as such is not a superficial phenomenon, as is clearly demonstrated by the rays of light emanating from a light source. An impression of a luminous surface can be achieved with conventional illuminants by using appropriate reflector and diffuser technology, as well as a multiple arrangement of light sources. Creating and using artificial light-emitting surfaces is now, however, a viable option: this is attributable to the development of OLEDs (organic light-emitting diodes) and luminous films. Intelligent luminous surfaces (daylight and artificial light-reflecting or artificial light-emitting surfaces) appear nonetheless to be long-established in an architectural context.

Ever larger applications of media façades are becoming widespread, with recent designs covering not merely façades, but entire city districts. ill. Light.17.1, p. 46

1
The optical technologies unite technologies involving the medium of light. See Federal Ministery of Education and Research (2002), Optical Technology.
2
Reason enough for the European Commission to phase it out, starting in 2009. See EU Directive concerning lighting products in private households 12/2008.

The intelligence of these projects lies less in the luminous surfaces than in the combination of illuminants and associated control systems used to display images on oversized monitors.

ill. Light.10.2, p. 24 The lighting technology involved is generally LED-based and is therefore composed of a large number of minute dots of light. Depending on the density of the illuminants (fluorescent tubes, LED), a more-or-less sharp, plane image surface is created, which can be optimised by the additional integration of reflectors and diffusers. High resolution screens, however, often do not entirely fulfil the expectations raised by the term 'media façade'. Whereas other high-tech surfaces seem to integrate diverse structural-physical and visual requirements in one material as a matter of course, the technology in most media façades appears very dated. These structures are often closed at the back, thereby completely cutting off the rooms behind the façade from lighting and ventilation. Technological innovations such as transparent films fitted with LEDs, or ultra-light constructions, indicate the much-needed development potential offered by hybrid designs. The combination of complete transparency and optimal visibility striven for with LEDs seems to have been achieved for the first time by the integration of invisible conductors in glass. Prototypes are currently being introduced to the market. The LEDs are embedded in a cast resin composite between two panes, with a quasi-wireless power supply (via transparent conductors integrated in the laminated glass).

ill. Light.06.1, p. 15 Another advantage of this technology is that the light can, if required, be emitted in both directions, towards the inside as well as the outside.

Stanislaw Lem, Solaris, p. 202 f.

I went closer, and when the next wave came I held out my hand. What followed was a faithful reproduction of a phenomenon which had been analyzed a century before: the wave hesitated, recoiled, then enveloped my hand without touching it, so that a thin covering of 'air' separated my glove inside a cavity which had been fluid a moment previously, and now had a fleshy consistency.

In view of their primary use in public spaces, there arises the question of the cultural significance of media façades in the future, as compared to other mass media such as radio, television or the Internet. What other options are offered by light-emitting or kinetic surfaces? Beyond the actual intention, irrespective of whether the contents are of a purely artistic, commercial or atmospheric nature, media façades always aim to attract attention. There is, of course, no doubt about the fascination radiated by large, flickering surfaces. In this context—and entirely in the sense of Guy Debord's cultural critique The Society of the Spectacle (1967)[3]—the quality of light is of a spectacular nature, in continuation of the tradition of outdoor advertising. The number of media façades is increasing rapidly: a kind of 'illumination arms race' as it were, with as yet unforeseeable consequences for urban environments and their inhabitants. In 2007, the mayor of São Paolo imposed an advertising ban on the entire city, which had a huge impact on the urban façades then covered by large posters and advertising hoardings.

2 Light nuances

In the past, the chief purpose of outdoor lighting was to ensure visibility and orientation at night, generally directly linked to safety and security concerns,[4] whereas today, the effects of light and shade on structures and the theatrical effect of architectural surfaces are gaining increasing attention. Many cities make use of coordinated lighting design concepts,[5] in which different qualities of light[6] are integrated as a matter of course. The growing number of large-area media façades gives rise to many issues worthy of consideration. The term 'light emission' is becoming especially important in this respect. Light radiating out into the night without usefully illuminating anything does not add value and is not sustainable. In addition to the negative influence of such light on the physiological systems of living creatures, the concomitant loss of the night sky is a problem not only for astronomers, whose telescopic images are overexposed, owing to the excessive background light emitted by cityscapes: the ability to perceive the subtle nuances of a landscape at dusk, or at night, is in danger of being lost. The Japanese writer Tanizaki Jun'ichiro describes the beauty of Japanese interiors, entirely based on the gradation of shadow and light, using shadow for an aesthetic purpose, in his book 'In Praise of Shadows'.[7] The ability to perceive these nuances is a prerequisite for appreciating such rooms. A sensibility for 'the mystery of shadow', NANO Technical Background 5, p.83 however, also appears to be growing in western cultural environments. The integration of shade in the light façade of the Centre of Contemporary Art in Cordoba, for example, is an important feature. ill. Light.02.2, p.30; Light.02, p.163 In conventional light façades, the changes between day, night, and night time periods of restricted use are problematic. The façade developed for the museum incorporates a daytime effect too: the shadow play achieved with relief panels of various sizes and differing arrangement creates a 'living' façade in sunlight. As it gets dark, the relief panels become the individual pixels of

3
"When the real world is transformed into mere images, mere images become real beings—dynamic figments that provide the direct motivations for a hypnotic behaviour."
Debord (1967), The Society of the Spectacle, p.19.

4
See Schievelbusch (1983), Bright Spots.

5
e.g. Plan Lumière Zurich: By identifying and concentrating on significant intervention zones in urban environments, a composition is created by the formation of individual light ensembles, allowing a coherent experience of these public areas. The inclusion of less well illuminated zones is also important in this respect.
Stadt Zürich (2004), Plan Lumière.

6
Richard Kelly, the first to break away from the specification of a uniform lighting intensity as a central lighting design criterion, differentiated between three ways of using light: ambient light—light for seeing (better); focal glow—light for drawing attention; play of brilliance—light for looking at, light that is there solely to be looked at itself.
See Kelly (1952), Lighting.

7
Jun'ichiro (1987), Lob des Schattens [In Praise of Shadows], p.33.

a media façade, continuing the light effects from the inside as film sequences. The identity of night and day is emphasised by the black-and-white aesthetic of the façade.

Although light and shade are also very important for kinetic media façades, these are not light façades in a real sense. The appearance of the façade is determined by the gradations of

light, rather than the light colour and pixel density. **ill. Light.03.2, p. 24; ill. Light.15.1, p. 33;** INFORMATION Technical Background 2.1, p. 146; **Light.03, p. 166** The façade panels can be given different inclinations using telescopic rods, causing their surfaces to reflect to a corresponding extent and thus generating patterns, shapes or information. The flowing movement of the kinetic components creates a highly poetic play of light and shade. Since the degree to which they reflect ambient light depends on the angle of incidence, the elements become large and surprisingly playful reflectors.

The fact that appropriate and intelligent illumination can improve architecture as well as create spectacular effects is undisputed. Yet light, the immaterial component, is only rarely used specifically for surface design. It is surprising that more attention is not paid to light-controlling and reflective surfaces in architecture, when one considers how important reflectors, for example, are in lighting design and how easily an effect similar to using reflectors could be achieved by treating the surfaces of a building.

Reflector technology, in addition to illuminants and colour filters, has always been a core research area. Nanotechnology-based developments NANO Technical Background 3, p. 75 have made it possible to create reflectors that are high-precision instruments for distributing and directing light. Coatings applied in a vacuum environment, for instance, allow the specific optimisation of reflector materials, allowing them to withstand the significant deformation to which they are subjected during manufacturing. The latest precise reflector designs are based on dividing reflector surfaces into individual segments. In contrast to conventionally faceted reflectors, these individual surfaces are not

flat, but three-dimensional and spherically curved. **ill. Light.13.2, p. 32** Depending on the surface, the incident light can be bundled specifically, scattered in a controlled manner, or reflected.

An extraordinary lighting experience can be created using a three-dimensional structure, something the designers of the

Cocoon Club have already made use of. **ill. Light.01.1, p. 26; Light.01, p. 162** The perforated wall surfaces of the main room are clearly reminiscent of a permeable cell membrane. The multi-layer construction and the

surface structure make this the most significant architectural element of the club. A moving 360° projection on the perforated wall can be coordinated in real time with the DJ set. The rather intoxicating effect of the room is achieved almost exclusively by an ingenious use of light. Guests experience a world with an artificially created atmosphere,[8] in an *immersive environment*.

The use of the term 'spectacular lighting' to describe these special light effects seems appropriate in this respect, since light is projected not only onto one wall, but all of them. Attention is drawn both to the room and to the guest. This type of spectacular lighting is obviously limited in terms of application. Luminous wallpaper, on the other hand, promises to be more suitable for everyday use. The typical three-dimensional light objects for-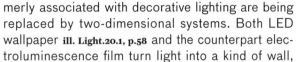merly associated with decorative lighting are being replaced by two-dimensional systems. Both LED wallpaper **ill. Light.20.1, p.58** and the counterpart electroluminescence film turn light into a kind of wall, and thus into an architectural component. Changing the appearance of interior and exterior walls at the push of a button is as surprising as it is effective and indicates how the appearance of OLEDs on the market could influence developments in the use of artificial light.

8
In this context, Reinhard Knodt talks about the phenomenon of the feast and the atmospheric flooding that takes place there and the decay of space and time. See Knodt (1994), Ästhetische Korrespondenzen, p.50.

1 Photonics

Although Edison's invention of the electric light bulb in 1879 enjoyed a lot of public attention, innovations in the lighting technology sector go largely unnoticed nowadays. Developments are generally only followed by experts involved in the field. Yet lighting technology is a key technology for many innovations. These include applications in areas such as the health sector, traffic and environment, communications and production engineering, as well as biotechnology and nanoelectronics. 'Photonics' is an new term incorporating the words 'photon' and 'electronics', reflecting the objective of optical engineering 'to complete as many tasks as possible with light—i.e. using photons'.[1] The study of lighting engineering (illuminants, lighting management) is a broad field. Energy equivalent to several billion euros a year could be saved by introducing new technological developments. Modern *light-emitting diodes* (LEDs), for instance, are not only more compact than other illuminants, but can also be controlled electronically, have a low surface temperature, variable emission angles and long service life, as well as being virtually maintenance-free and requiring very little energy. Although the full impact of new lighting developments resulting from of light engineering research is not yet clear, experts agree that they will bring about a fundamental change in our use of lighting. When innovative, energy-saving sources of light, or light-emitting surfaces, such as organic LEDs (OLEDs) become capable of illuminating with significantly greater efficiency and durability than conventional incandescent lamps or fluorescent tubes, they will give architects and designers a whole new range of possibilities in design. ill. Light.10.1, p.24 This will not, however, be due to the new illuminants alone. The dynamisation of artificial light by electronic control systems will soon play an equally important role in design.

1
See Federal Ministry of Education and Research (2002), Optical Technology, p.4.

2 Dynamic light

Although the light intensity of conventional lamps can be varied using dimmers and digital ballasts (e.g. DALI server),[2] INFORMATION Technical Background 2.4, p. 154 it takes semiconductor-based lamps (LED and OLED) to achieve virtually unlimited and continuously variable regulation of level and colour of lighting.[3] Such lighting systems were both exclusive and expensive until recently, but the mass production of affordable lighting management components is now opening up a broad spectrum of applications. Whereas animated media façades have been demonstrating the exterior potential of light at night for many years, the control of artificial light indoors is now becoming increasingly interesting. In addition to exploiting light aesthetically in interior design, fig. Light—Shadow, p. 108 it seems likely that artificial illumination can be managed and controlled so as to have a beneficial physical influence on people, thanks to more precise findings about the way in which the human organism is influenced by the light-dark cycle represented by day and night.[4] Light and colour constellations can have a positive and stimulating effect on the biorhythm of individuals, thereby improving general well-being and the quality of life.[5]

Intelligent light surfaces can be created in many different ways, as indicated below. A distinction is made between *light-emitting surfaces* (electroluminescent surfaces) and light surfaces made up of many individual luminaires—called *light surface systems* here. Examples of light surface systems are given in the section of this book on projects and images, while the technical principles of light-emitting surfaces are described below. Light-emitting diodes (LEDs) are special in the sense that these can be characterised both as the standard contemporary module of light

2
Lighting control devices based on a Digital Addressing Light Interface (DALI), which permits the targeted control of complex configurations of lighting technology devices. The DALI protocol is an established lighting technology standard in the building technology sector. It should be distinguished from the Digital Multiplex protocol (DMX), most commonly used in stage and event technology. "This open standard was established in Europe and has been adopted in North America, where mainstream applications are embracing it." See Berjansky (2004), Hello DALI as well as DALI Manual (2001).

3
Theoretically, up to 16.7 million colour variations can be set.

4
"Research results have shown that, in addition to the receptors responsible for vision (rods and cones), there are also biologically active receptors in our eyes. These influence the production of the hormones melatonin and cortisol. While melatonin makes a person sleepy and relaxed, cortisol makes individuals awake and active. This is why the way we feel in the course of a day changes, why we sleep at night and suffer from jet lag when we cross time zones", Van Bommel and van den Beld (2001), Industrial Lighting, pp. 14–15.

5
The circadian rhythm helps an organism to adjust to phenomena recurring on a daily basis. It is an important component of chronobiology and sleep research. The basic conditions of 'healthy' artificial light are described by Rea (2002), Light—Much more than Vision, pp. 1–15.

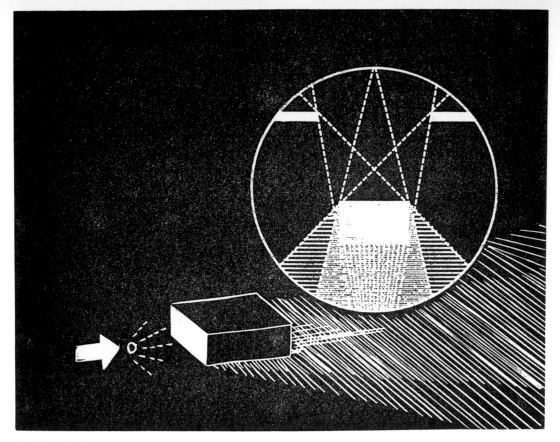

fig. Light—Shadow

surface systems and (on account of their almost microscopic size) as the components of additively assembled light-emitting surfaces. The main aspects of utilising these important illuminants, which are technically relatively simple, are also discussed.

3 Light surface systems

- Projection surfaces: the projection of light onto space-enclosing walls, or the building envelope, from a suitable distance (ranging from less than a metre to several hundred metres, depending on projector technology) using one or more projectors
- Rear projection surfaces: the projection of light from inside a building onto a translucent façade surface, using one or more projectors
- Display façades (very large screen video display): even distribution of addressable light dots (pixels) in front of or behind a façade, with appropriate regulation; the distance between pixels is generally

2–10 cm, exceptionally up to 100 cm. The display is also visible
during the day, depending on light intensity and dot pitch
• Window matrix, or room matrix animation: the utilisation of room
light, controlled via bus systems; each window or room corresponds
to one pixel
• Illuminated façades: illuminants between the glazing of double-skin
façades, controlled by bus systems; roller blinds or slatted blinds
serve as reflectors
• Mechanical façades / kinetic façades: the specifically directed reflection of daylight by electronically controlled mobile façade elements. **fig. Light – Reflection, p. 110**

3.1 LED as components of additive light-emitting surfaces
A basic LED is one of the simplest optoelectronic structural elements.
Just like the organic LEDs currently being intensively researched,
ordinary LEDs are semiconducting structural elements. The most important component is a semiconductor crystal that emits light when
charged with electricity. LEDs are therefore also electroluminescent
elements. Detailed documentation of the technology involved in LEDs
is broadly accessible, which is why only basic information is provided
here.[6] LEDs are characterised by a very long lifetime, robustness and
low energy consumption. Incandescent lamps convert as little as two
percent of the electrical power into light energy, whereas modern
LEDs have an efficiency of around 25 percent. Important parameters to be considered when using LEDs include design (construction, structural type), light colour (spectral characteristic) and radiant power, which is related to the aperture angle (emission angle).
Manufacturers classify LEDs using a BIN code, as well as a degree
of selectivity. This method of sorting LEDs is referred to as 'bin-
ning'. Since LEDs are point sources, the light emitted by them can
be directed precisely. Their immediate response to control impulses
makes them particularly suitable for the fast, dynamic light scenes
typical of media façades. The plastic encasement of the diode, which
is common to all structural types, functions both as protection and
as a lens, as well as codetermining the radiant power of
the LED. **ill. Light.10.2, p. 24** Since this decreases with increasing
temperature, LEDs should be in-
stalled away from direct sunlight
or other sources of heat.

[6]
For example http://en.wikipedia.org/
wiki/Light-emitting_diode,
and Ris (2008), **Practical Lighting
Technology.**

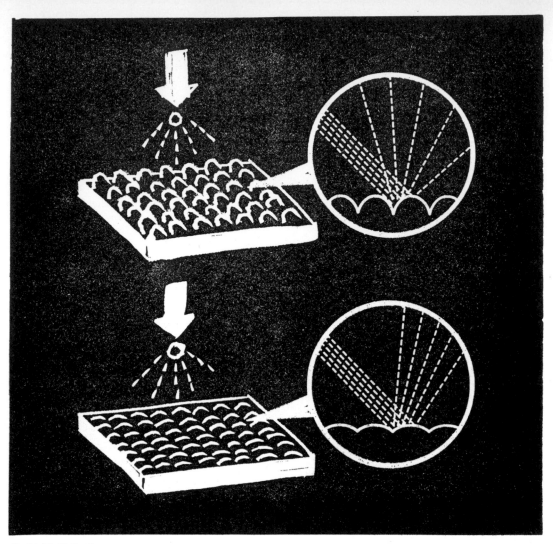

fig. Light—Reflection

The many types of LED available can be grouped into four categories. The characteristic T-type usually has a plastic housing of 3–5 mm enclosing the wired LED. The shape of the lens determines the light emission angle. As a light source with a low luminous flux, it is used as an orientation and signal luminaire. Another group consists of the *Surface Mounted Devices (SMD)*, in which the component is mounted directly on the circuit board 'from above' and soldered. The Chip on Board (COB) technology involves placing the chip directly on a circuit board without its own casing. *High Power LEDs* are LEDs with a power consumption of over 1 watt. This could apply to SMD or COB-type LEDs. Special construction to ensure very low thermal resistance between chip and circuit board is essential. The objectives currently determining the development of LEDs include more compact design, higher luminous flux, better luminous efficacy and more economical production. Another aim is the reduction of manufacturing-related colour tolerances.

LEDs emit light in a limited spectral range. This light is virtually monochromatic. It took quite some time to develop LEDs for each of the colours of the visible spectrum. The first LEDs, produced in 1962, were red, whereas blue LEDs have only been available since 1996. The production of white light still requires a considerable effort. The light of 'white' LEDs is obtained by the additive combination of differently coloured LEDs placed close to each other (blue/yellow or red/green/blue (RGB) combinations) or by mounting luminous substances in front of blue LEDs. The latter method is more common because it is cheaper. Such LEDs are characterised by the narrower bandwidth of the blue light range and by the broad spectral range of the luminous material.

The LED is a multi-facetted, relatively economical, easy-to-use, semi-finished product, which is suitable both for low-tech applications and for ambitious specialist design. It is the basic unit for calculating and building most media façades ('one LED is equivalent to one pixel') ill. Light.04.3, p. 21; Light.04, p. 168 and will replace the incandescent lamp as the standard illuminant in future.[7] Its different possible applications are discussed in numerous internet forums and blogs, while many imaginative applications are presented by individual designers, artists and creative communities.[8] LEDs are also a pop culture phenomenon.[9]

7
Electrodeless lamps represent an alternative technology with which microwave energy can be converted to visible light. Corresponding systems promise an energy saving potential of up to 50 percent compared to normal illuminants, coupled with higher luminous efficacy and a longer lifetime. Illuminants for architectural applications are in the process of development. See The Economist (2007), Illumination—Everlasting Light.

8
See for instance the internet forum blinkenlights.org, the name being derived from a German-English corruption of the word Blinklicht (literally 'flashing light' in the sense of an indicator light, or now LED) at US American universities in the 1950s. A standard has been set by the noncommercial, participative, media façade productions staged by a loose cooperation between the Blinkenlight group and the closely related blinkenarea.org in cities including Berlin, Paris and Toronto.

9
See the LED Throwies project by the Graffiti Research Lab (http://graffitiresearchlab.com) and Platt (2006), My Love Affair with LEDs, among others.

- Electroluminescence films
- Organic light-emitting diodes (OLEDs)

4.1 Electroluminescence films

Electroluminescent materials start to emit light when an electric field is applied to them. A thin film no thicker than 1 mm, made of electroluminescent material, (generally zinc sulphide doped with metals) is enclosed between two conducting layers (electrodes). The light-emitting material has to be separated from the two electrodes either by additional insulating layers, or by embedding microparticles in an insulating matrix. If only one of these layers is pervious to light, a reflecting layer can be added to the other (non-translucent) layer to achieve a higher luminous efficacy. The whole illuminant structure made of plastic foils is normally only a few millimetres thick. A typical form of application is Thin Film Electroluminescence (TFEL), ill. **Light.05.1, p. 54; Light.05, p. 173** in which the electroluminescent and insulating coatings are applied by screen printing, which explains why the term 'printable light' is also used. A basic pigment material in which the zinc sulphide molecules are micro-encapsulated already exists. In this case, the luminance is, however, reduced a little and is not quite as homogenous, owing to the larger distance between the molecules. Such EL films are extremely thin, highly flexible and economical and they can be cut. These material properties and production methods, particularly those of electroluminescent pastes (EL pastes), are being examined for new design applications, increasingly also experimentally.[10] ill. **Light.20.1, p. 58;** INFORMATION Technical Background 2.3, p. 152 The light has low proportions of UV and IR light, as well as being flicker-free and non-reflective. The robust and almost freely bendable films can luminesce in various colours, with the light of coloured films always appearing to be more intense than that of white ones. The colour effects can be created directly in the film, or by using filter foils. Electroluminescent films have a lifetime of at least 10,000 hours. They are not suitable for illuminating rooms because of their characteristically low luminance. Electroluminescent films are primarily used for backlighting displays, or for advertising. Their advantages

[10] See Neudeck and Thurner (2008), Luminescent Compounds. The development of EL pastes lies behind a pioneering field of research called 'printed electronics'. See Arning and Steiger (2008), Printed Electronics.

include contour accuracy and good long-distance visibility of large areas of non-directional light. Architectural applications are becoming more widespread: as emergency and night lights; as components of guiding systems; as luminous floor graphics and decorative interior and exterior luminous surfaces, as well as in exhibition and trade fair design.

4.2 Organic light-emitting diodes—OLEDs

Organic light-emitting diodes are based on an alternative, very powerful technology that was initially developed for displays. OLEDs could be described as luminous plastics. Just like conventional LEDs, OLEDs are semiconductor elements that emit light upon the application of electric voltage. ill. Light.07.1, p.19 OLEDs are therefore also electroluminescent elements. The underlying physical mechanism, however, differs from the way in which electroluminescent films work. Although OLED technology was originally developed as an alternative display technology for computers and mobile phones, it is increasingly firing the imagination of lighting designers and architects. Among the advantages over conventional liquid crystal displays (LCDs) are more brilliant colours, high luminous intensity and the use of very thin—and soon also flexible—elements in designs. OLEDs have been used in monochromatic graphic displays, such as those used in car radios, for some time. The low operating voltage required makes them ideal for use in battery-powered devices.

Although OLEDs can be manufactured using a diversity of organic materials and various methods, the fundamental principle is always the same. The simplest form of organic light-emitting diode consists of a semiconductive, organic, ultra-thin film of conjugated polymers (i.e. polymers that are luminescent on account of their specific atomic structure), enclosed by two electrodes: one transparent translucent anode and a metallic cathode reflecting the light produced in the OLED. When current flows through this sandwich, negatively charged electrons move from the cathode to the organic film. In the meantime, positive charges, called 'holes', are generated by the anode. Electrons and holes move towards each other, ideally meeting in the middle of the OLED film. In the course of this, their charges are neutralised, they recombine and the energy released in the process is emitted in the form of photons, i.e. light. If an OLED has two layers (2-layer OLED), the recombination behaviour can be optimised and the effectiveness of the OLED increased. The name refers to two thin polymer films, a hole transport layer and an electron transport layer. fig. OLED, p.115 An emitter or recombination layer is located between these two layers. Depending on the type, this is partially or wholly composed of specific colouring materials, therefore determining the OLED colour. The element is no thicker than 200 nm (0.2 thousandths of a millimetre) altogether.[11] Most research currently taking place can be understood with reference to the principal construction of single and double-layer OLEDs. Multi-layer OLEDs, for instance, are part of a strategy of improving device efficiency by combining layers, whereas the characteristic feature of transparent OLEDs (TOLEDs) is a transparent cathode. Pixel-precise control of displays can be achieved by the integration of ultra-thin matrices and shadow masks. The production of small molecule LEDs (SMOLEDs) and polymer LEDs (PLEDs) represents two current methods of manufacturing OLEDs: SMOLEDs are made by the vacuum deposition of small, light-emitting molecules. This method is still relatively expensive and complicated. The second method uses long-chain plastics, or polymers. These large molecules can be dissolved in liquid. The solution is then applied or propelled on to the electrodes by means of spin coating, a microtechnology-based coating technique for producing uniform thin films, or else by using a type of inkjet printer. Although PLEDs are significantly cheaper to manufacture than SMOLEDs, PLEDs are still subject to the drawback that different colours have different lifetimes. Research into finding materials to solve this problem is in progress. Chemical variability allows OLEDs to be produced in virtually every colour. Using the thin film system, they can be applied to large areas of flexible substrate. Because of their extreme sensitivity to moisture and oxygen, the diodes still have to be encapsulated in glass.

Although a number of problems still need to be solved, OLEDs are considered to be the most significant lighting technology of the future. OLEDs are already being used for some smaller types of display area and the market maturity of large area applications is imminent, with a billion dollar market predicted for 2011 alone. Emitting

[11] See also Brütting and Rieß (2008), **Grundlagen organischer Halbleiter.** OLED technology is a steadily developing research area. Begun in October 2008, the OLED-100.eu project is the follow-up to the European Union's 2004 OLLA research project into OLED technologies. Numerous further links are provided on the web site of the same name (see http://oled100.eu). Up-to-date information is provided at Leo (2009), OLED Q&A.

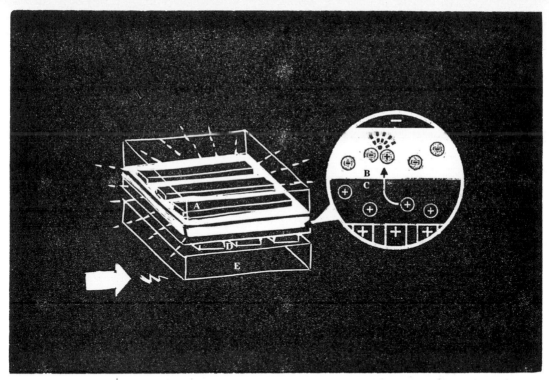

fig. OLED
A = cathode, B = emitter polymer, C = conductive polymer, D = anode, E = transparent glass plate

light from their entire surface, OLEDs ideally complement the point sources of light represented by LEDs in the field of lighting design. The fact that ultra-thin, controllable, real surfaces of light are involved will give rise to a fundamental change in lighting use. According to the latest research reports, it will soon be possible to make OLEDs that are transparent when switched off. This would allow ultra-thin, transparent and flexible light films to be applied to all sorts of surface. The extreme thinness of the material required, coupled with the even emission of light from the surface, would then make any given surface a potential lighting substrate. Further development of this light-emitting material would provide a film-like luminous material that could be used for designing structural skins. Architects and designers would gain new inspiration for atmospheric environments and impressive presentations if every wall and ceiling area could be illuminated at the press of a button: glass panes might begin to glow subtly at dusk, or display panels could suddenly become visible. This might sound a little like scenes from a science fiction film at the moment, but it could become reality in a few years time.

CLIMATE Discourse

1 Climate-regulating surfaces

It first has to be said that no study of the design potential of climate-regulating surfaces and the climate design of shells and façades is complete without reference to the extensive background parameters. The representations of those global changes, for which Bruce Mau has coined the essentially liberating formula *Massive Change* discussed in the introductory chapter have culminated in a debate about climate, supported by a wealth of statistics[1] and influenced by numerous lobby groups, which has been continuing for quite some time. This approach explicitly interprets practical constraints as representing options for action in the field of design (and architecture).[2] Within this field, the necessity of using material resources responsibly and of climate-conscious, energy-efficient building is not fundamentally in question. In the ongoing debate, rather ethical-moral, holistic viewpoints *(green building)* correlate loosely with approaches based on economic good sense *(saving energy costs)* and engineering efficiency (passive house), which have, on balance, become the yardstick for legislation and technical standards. Departures from a conventional mindset committed to economic growth, which one might actually expect, are not always immediately discernible.[3] As a result, architecture and design, the 'original meaning'[4] of which includes the design of climate shells (clothing, walls, façades) have, rather surprisingly, arrived at a point where extensive regulation, ill-defined directives and a wealth of standardised industrial building products tend to restrict rather than expand freedom of action.[5] The necessary breakthrough to the level of creative action formulated by Mau is supported by strong, conceptually open positions. Among the select few ideas of importance in architecture are the characterisation of the shell as a skin,[6] in the tradition of anthropomorphising architectural analogies,

1
See International Energy Agency, Key World Energy Statistics, www.iea.org.

2
"Massive Change is a celebration of our global capacities, but also a cautious look at our limitations." Mau (2004), Massive Change.

3
See "The 10 Dumbest Green Buildings on Earth" a list of buildings which have been LEED-certified by the U.S. Green Building Council (USGBC), which includes, among others, a filling station. LEED stands for Leadership in Energy and Environmental Design. The Green Building movement reflects the comparatively new trend towards sustainable building in the USA.
See http://greenbuildingelements.com/2009/02/16/the-10-dumbest-green-buildings-on-earth.

4
See Hausladen et al. (2008), Climate Skin.

5
See the EU Directive on the energy performance of buildings (2002/91/EG) and the Energy Saving Ordinance EnEV which applies in Germany, which requires that proof of a building's energy consumption be provided (energy performance certificate). Its amendment in mid-2009 and that planned for 2012 are intended to lead to savings of 30 percent in each case. See www.enev.de.

6
On the history of its meaning in architecture, see Benthien (2001), Haut [Skin], pp. 33–39. The outermost limit, in a double sense, is marked by the Planetary Skin project, initiated by the US space agency NASA and well-known IT companies, which is intended to collect data from a world-wide monitoring system of satellites and sensor networks and make it available online.
See www.planetaryskin.org.

and its idealisation as a capsule,[7] which draws on the technical-poetic tradition. Both cases involve repeatedly used (but essentially individually specified) metaphors, adapted to the relevant position, from which are derived nonetheless (or for this very reason) numerous approaches to both the 'classic' and the 'experimental' climatic design of shells and surfaces.

2 Skin or capsule

The skin is used as a metaphor for boundaries and as the ultimate symbol of surface. With his characterisation of the house as a second skin that expands our range of senses, Michel Serres perhaps expresses most clearly this frequently cited topos of clothing, or the shell of a building, as an important synthetic extension which helps us relate to our environment.[8] As the largest human organ, the skin, with its sensory organs, supplies direct information about the environment: "The skin reads the texture, weight density and temperature of matter... Home and pleasure of the skin turn into a singular sensation."[9] Comparisons with the skin can already be found in Alberti, who described layers of plaster as the skin of the body of the house. There is a fascination in its seemingly indefinable visual and haptic qualities and its ability to react to climatic changes in the environment. In this respect, Oxman and Hart's concept of *Construction in Vivo* (already described in the Nano chapter) comes very close to the ideal of the skin as a living, homogeneous,

permeable biomembrane. ill. Nano.03.3, p. 29; NANO Discourse 4, p. 72; Nano.03, p.163 The genealogy of useful comparisons ranges from the concept of the skin as a structure pervaded by vessels ill. Climate.18.1, p. 55 (which applies, among other things, to the thermally-activated building systems, or TABS, which will be described in the following section) and the comparison of the layers of the skin with functional layers in building physics, to the classic characterisation of the shell and supporting structure as the 'skin and bones' of a building.[10] CLIMATE Technical Background 3, p. 127 The ideal of the climate shell as a second skin is expressed in the vision of the Living Building, which the building physicist and proponent of the Green Building, Jason F. McLennan, describes as a synthetic ecological subsystem adapted to the particular circumstances and the changing climatic conditions of its location, capable of generating the resources required for its operation (water, heat, electrical energy) itself. In doing so, it should not produce any harmful emissions, its waste products should be fully recycled, and not only should it not cause damage to the local ecosystem, but it should positively influence and strengthen it.[11]

7
The history of the manifestations of the capsule, from da Vinci to the Viennese visionaries of the 1970s and up to the present, is outlined by Feuerstein (2000), Cell and Capsule.
8
Benthien (2001), Haut [Skin], p. 38.
9
See Pallasmaa (2008), p.57, p. 59.
10
A current interpretation is offered by Hodge (2006), Skins + Bones.
11
McLennan, Berkebile (1999), The Living Building.

The capsule is the counter concept to the skin. This concept is based on the assumption of a marked divergence between two immediately adjacent climatic zones, which needs to be controlled. From a technical viewpoint, the capsule logically finds its determining expression in the principle of insulation, given that the associated verb form means to 'disassociate, isolate, seal off'.[12] The manner in which it functions is illustrated by those typical building physics diagrams of wall structures, in which the connection between an essentially constant interior and a continuously changing exterior is represented by rising or descending polylines, which thus provide information on the physical (and not, as in the case of the skin, the quasi-biological) behaviour of the system. With this method of calculation, the capsule makes habitation a calculated risk, even in climatically difficult-to-extreme environments. However, its actual focus is on the interior. Capsules are an expression of individuality and an assertion of social community.[13] They make it possible to create prototypical, ideal, model living spaces. To the extent that they imply that these alien worlds could exist outside, too, they are harbingers of the utopian. They protect the artificial heritage of the garden of Eden. Not without reason does the genealogy of the capsule include the conservatories and greenhouses of the nineteenth century, Buckminster Fullers' geodesic domes and the fleet of biotope arks floating in space in the visionary film *Silent Running*:[14] *Yes, we build spaceships.*[15] The spaceship, as perhaps the ultimate form of the capsule, is the opposite of an escapist vision. The idea of the spaceship conveys an awareness of boundaries.[16] It stands both for the ecological problem and for a sceptical faith in technology.

As ideals, the skin symbolises the openness of a system, the capsule its fundamentally closed nature. Though helpful as a model assumption, from an ecological viewpoint neither extreme is logically conceivable when applied to biological systems. In fact, the permeability of the shell essentially defines the degree of interrelationship between system and environment. This degree of interconnection determines its fundamental viability, irrespective of the state of the art, culture and control over nature: we maintain ourselves as closed systems by being open systems.[17] In biological systems, the degree of interconnection of a membrane is developed during the course of evolution. In terms of the design of synthetic climate-regulating surfaces, there is a certain challenge in reconciling the design idea with the findings of modern building physics

12
See Wahrig Dictionary of Foreign Words, current edition.

13
The study of political-cultural alternative designs of the 1960s and 70s in the USA by Felicity D. Scott shows the capsule (spherical shells, geodesic domes) as the architectural *Leitmotiv* of alternative environments. See Scott (2007), Architecture or Techno-utopia.

14
Its real-life equivalent, Biosphere II, with its five model ecosystems in the desert of Arizona, is for science journalist Florian Rötzler a 'transitional solution'. See Rötzler (1997), Virtueller Raum oder Weltraum? p.380.

15
"We are space travellers on earth, what we do is deliberately assemble the unknown." Oosterhuis (2002), We build spaceships. The text, presented in the form of a fictitious interview, describes the spaceship as a poetic design strategy.

16
See Fuller (1963), Operating Manual for Spaceship Earth.

17
"We will never be able to become one with nature, open ourselves up, allow ourselves to be permeated, gently smile, close our eyes [...] we would be extinguished. We can never rigidly cut ourselves off from nature, maintain our identity at any price, encapsulate ourselves, inflate ourselves [...] we would burst with a gigantic bang." Eisenhardt et al. (1995), Wie Neues entsteht, pp. 75–76. See also Reichholt (2008), "Only functioning imbalances can make 'sustainable developments' possible", p.137.

research.[18] CLIMATE Technical Background 4, p 129. Building physics, as an engineering science dealing with complex interrelationships, starts out by determining the spatial dimensions of climate zones (macroclimates, mesoclimates, microclimates). Its purpose is the objective climatic evaluation of building geometries, constructions and building materials. As a discipline, it is caught between the massive changes which are taking place at one level and simplistic model assumptions at another. The problem with climate design is, in part, its strong emphasis on the big picture, even bearing in mind that the big debates are reflected in the pioneering character of holistic concepts such as that of the *Living Building*. The concepts of skin and capsule outlined here should not be misunderstood in this exclusive sense. They refer both to the valuable simulative design strategies of bionics, biomimetics[19] and bioconstructivism[20] on the one hand, and to the ideology-free, prototypically experimental investigation of partial aspects on the other, which are becoming increasingly important in the area of information-communicating surfaces, for example. INFORMATION Technical Background 3, p.155 Big ideas are interesting when they give rise to diversity and stimulate dialogue.

18
"The façade of a building forms the interface between the environment and the user inside [...] the requirements (imposed on it) lead to conflicting goals." See Hausladen et al. (2008), Climate Skin, p.151.

19
See ACADIA 08 (2008), Silicon + Skin, Proceedings.

20
See Mertins (2004), Bioconstructivism.

CLIMATE Technical Background

1 Climate simulations

Beyond the necessity of providing protection against the inclemencies of the weather, climate design proves to be a task of high complexity, the singularities of which are reflected in language. An American-Japanese collective of artists and engineers, *Experiments in Art and Technology (E.A.T.)*, responded to the non-specific commission to design a prestigious corporate pavilion for PepsiCo at the World Exposition in Osaka in 1970 with the idea of a large walk-in sculpture of fog and light: "Laughingly, but with a serious intention, the artists thought that the best pavilion would be no pavilion at all. An ideal solution would have been a pavilion that could disappear. [...] The Fog became the symbolic guide to the concept of the Pavilion."[1] This summary by the Japanese artist Fujiko Nakaya, daughter of a well-known climate researcher, who was commissioned to design the fog, expresses the difficulties involved in defining judgment criteria for the technical solution: "Ample fog was the only way I could describe it [...] my most important decision was to choose real water fog for the pavilion."[2] This radical concept and its implementation illustrate the particular issues associated with the design of climate shells, which involve acting locally with material in the omnipresence of an immaterial phenomenon. With its envelope of fog and the large reflective dome inside it imitating the sun, together with sound installations, reflections and light effects, the Pepsi pavilion is a dematerialised paraphrase of the emblem of the preceding Expo in Montreal, Buckminster Fuller's geodesic dome. A work of architecture without architetural expression, as a walk-in artificial environment it is the most complete realisation of a building simulation. This term refers to one of the most important design methods, which displays a particular variety of facets in the field of climate design.

1
See Pearce (1972), An Architect's View, pp. 256 – 57.

2
See Nakaya (1972), The Making of Fog, p. 224.

Climate simulation is a design method, an instrument used in engineering science for acquisition of knowledge, a technological strategy and a global model.[3]

Methodologically speaking, built models ranging from the small, partial model up to the full-sized façade model make it possible to study 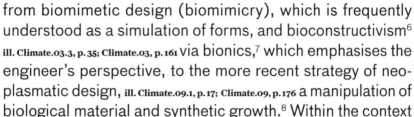 lighting conditions, shading and the principles of light guidance. ill. Nano.01.2, p. 52; ill. Nano.14.1, p. 31; Nano.01, p. 160 Simulations of air movement are also possible using wind tunnels. Already an integrated component of some CAD programs,[4] computer simulation allows complete time-based modelling of the climate behaviour of building components and of buildings themselves. Computer simulation has encouraged design strategies which postulate an orientation to the natural:[5] the bandwidth ranges from biomimetic design (biomimicry), which is frequently understood as a simulation of forms, and bioconstructivism[6] ill. Climate.03.3, p. 35; Climate.03, p. 161 via bionics,[7] which emphasises the engineer's perspective, to the more recent strategy of neoplasmatic design, ill. Climate.09.1, p. 17; Climate.09, p. 176 a manipulation of biological material and synthetic growth.[8] Within the context of the possibilities for analysis opened up by computer-assisted climate models, particulate sensor networks INFORMATION Technical Background 2.1, p. 146 and satellite-based monitoring systems (Global Information Systems— GIS) offer interesting new means of visually representing processes with which planning, from regional developments down to individual buildings, can be speculatively extrapolated.[9] In technological terms, the few innovations specifically relating to the climate behaviour of surfaces and envelopes can be understood as a simulation of the properties of heavy, massive components under the conditions of lightweight construction. Simulation and innovation in material technology require the refinement of proven principles of climate design (for example the redefinition of the interplay of light guidance and solar protection with the functional principles of heat-storing surfaces) and yield new conceptions of climate shells in the categories of skin and capsule.

3
A current view of the concept is offered by (2008), Simulation.

4
See http://ecotect.com.

5
Mertins (2004), Bioconstructivism.

6
See Beesley and Bonnemaison (2008), On Growth and Form. And Mertins (2007), Bioconstructivism.

7
Nachtigall (2002), Bionik für Ingenieure und Naturwissenschaftler.

8
See Cruz, Pike (2003), Neoplasmatic Design. And Oksiuta (2003), Spatium Gelatum.

9
Schmidt et al. (2007), Exposing New Orleans.

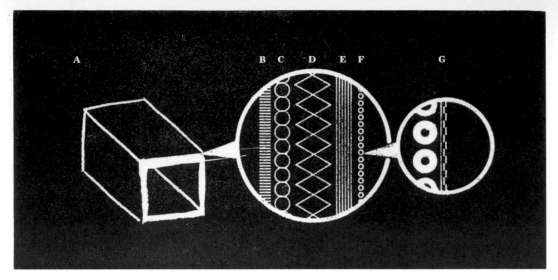

fig. Layer principle
A = covering, B = weather layer, C = air layer, D = insulating layer, E = structural layer, F = functional layer, G = coating

2 Material simulations

The building physics concept of layered construction has had a big impact on the design of climate shells. The 'ideal wall' describes the typical wall construction as a sequence of functional layers for the control of light, sound, rain, air, vapour, cold and heat in order to protect the structure and the interior of the building (reference to Illustration layers).[10] fig. Layer principle, p. 122 Innovations are aimed at developing the wall, as a complete system, in terms of the interaction of functional layers, and at increasing the efficiency of individual layers while reducing the amount of material used (reduction of thickness of layers).

2.1 Phase change materials

Buildings with exposed solid components (clay or brick walls, concrete ceilings) are characterised by a room climate which is perceived as being pleasant, which is essentially attributable to their heat-storing behaviour. In the same way as massive building components, thin layers charge latent heat storage elements (Phase Change Materials PCM) with thermal energy during the day, without significantly changing temperature of the latter, and release it again at night. fig. PCM, p. 123 This functional principle allows

10
"In concept, the perfect wall has the rainwater control layer, the air control layer, the vapor control layer and the thermal control layer on the exterior of the structure. The cladding's function is principally to act as an ultra-violet screen. [...] The physics of walls, roofs and slabs are conceptually the same."
See Lstiburek (2007), The Perfect Wall, pp. 74–75.

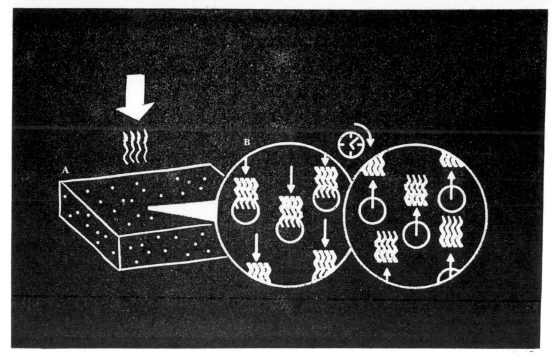

fig. PCM
A = material with PCM added, B = paraffin spheres (microcapsules)

a regulated ventilation of the interior, balancing out heat surpluses alternately between day and night. Typical, highly efficient PCMs include the wax paraffins. ill. Climate.12.1, p.14 They change from a solid state into a fluid state and back again, and their melting temperature can be adjusted. Optimistic calculations equate the reactive behaviour of a 2 cm thick layer of PCM plaster on a lightweight, massless plasterboard wall with that of an 18 cm thick concrete wall.[11] A distinction is made between passive systems, such as these, and active systems in which the heat stored in PCMs is transferred directly into another medium (e.g. water), ill. Climate.19.1, p.58 as a result of which the PCMs cool again more quickly. Active PCM systems allow several charging cycles per day and can react more quickly to fluctuations in the room climate. In principle, they can also be classed with the thermoactive building components (TAB) described below, which behave in a similar way.

11
See Kaltenbach (2005), PCM Latent
Heat Storage.

In order for them to retain their form and to prevent them from reacting with other materials, PCMs must be encapsulated, or bound. When microencapsulated, ill. Climate.11.1, p.14 they can be incorporated in plasterboard or plaster, as a conventional aggregate would be.

Macroencapsulation, on the other hand, allows the PCM to expand within the envelope. One example is a façade element filled with pure paraffin,[12] ill. Climate.15.1, p.45 the transmittance of which changes from roughly transparent to translucent, depending on the charging level. Macroencapsulated PCMs in pouches, metal boxes or dimpled sheet membranes allow uncomplicated subsequent installation in the form of suspended cooling ceilings, or as off-the-roll sheeting. Current research into PCMs is aimed at improving the efficiency and environmental compatibility of the components (material and envelope) and the adjustability of the melting point, as well as developing innovative systems, for example the combination of PCMs with vacuum insulation panels.[13]

2.2 Vacuum insulation and insulation materials
Considerable energy-saving effects can be achieved by optimising building insulation to reduce heat loss. Particular attention is therefore paid to thermal insulation materials. The various materials and systems in existence need to be evaluated in terms of thermal conductivity, diffusion properties and fire behaviour, service life, environmental compatibility and costs. The range of materials now available includes environmentally friendly ones (e.g. cellulose pellets) and highly pressure-resistant, moisture-insensitive (e.g. cellular glass) ones. Nonetheless, the choice of suitable insulation material remains a search for the compromise best suited to a particular context. Owing to its unusual properties, nanoporous aerogel is of particular importance. This super-lightweight, semi-transparent material, which is produced using metal oxides, polymers or carbons, ill. Nano.12.1, p.26 consists of up to 95 per cent air. It insulates noise and heat six times more effectively than conventional insulating materials and has extraordinary fire protection properties.[14] The tendency towards the use of increasingly large wall cross sections, in order to increase the

12
See Wymann (2004),
Wasserdurchströmtes Glas.
13
Ahmad et al. (2006),
Coupling VIP and PCM.
14
Fricke (2005),
From Dewars to VIP.

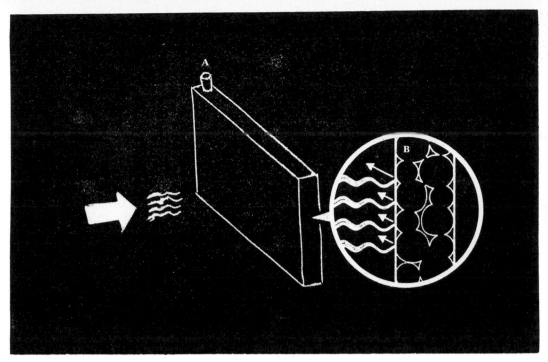

fig. Vacuum insulation panel
A = evacuation valve, B = packing material to stabilise the form/vacuum

insulating effect, is countered by vacuum insulation systems (VIS). These use a vacuum[15] to restrict the principal transmission path for heat via air (gas conduction). This operating principle is particularly efficient and therefore allows smaller system cross sections. With the same layer thickness, a vacuum insulation panel (VIP) is five-to-ten times more effective than conventional insulation materials. The different variants of VIPs are similar in their basic structure: a core made of a completely open-pored and thus evacuable material (e.g. polyurethane foam), which provides stability of form, enclosed in a gas barrier envelope. **fig. Vacuum insulation panel, p. 125** Composite plastic films and metal sheeting can be used as envelope material. The structure is varied through the use of glass fibres, glass-fibre-reinforced microporous silica, or aerogels (nanogel) for the core and the use of glass for the envelope. Another variant is vacuum insulation glass[16] (VIG), a relatively new product, which makes it unnecessary to fill the space between the panes with either inert gases or the aforementioned materials. In this case, however, damage to the envelope can lead to air entering the system and thus to the loss of the insulating effect. This handicap is the

15
See Tenpierik, Cauberg (2006), VIP. Friend or Foe?

16
See Weinläder et al. (2005), VIG Vacuum Insulation Glass.

most important criterion in the conception of suitable applications and constructive solutions. The use of the VIS therefore requires precise planning. Monitoring systems which measure the internal pressure of VIPs by means of sensors INFORMATION Technical Background 2.2, p. 150 are currently being investigated. Innovations are aimed at improving the envelope and core, the thermal bridges at the edges of joints and

the variety of form variants ill. Climate.17.2, p. 53 of the systems, as well as refining the construction. Among other things, the potential of prefabricated concrete VIP components and lightweight construction component systems is being

investigated.[17] ill. Climate.08.2, p. 59; Climate.08, p. 172 Other interesting approaches are offered by transparent thermal insulation (TTI) and multi-layer insulation (MLI). A complete TTI system consists of translucent honeycomb or hollow chamber structures, made of glass or plastics, located in front of a heat-absorbing wall (picture reference). Incident sunlight can reach the wall, where it is transformed into heat which, owing to the insulating effect of the TTI, for the most part flows into the interior of the building. As well as being used in combination with a wall, the TTI can also be used like opaque glazing.[18] Multi-layer insulation (MLI) is a thermal insulation material primarily used in space flight technology. It consists of a number (anything from a few up to several dozen) of layers of metallised plastic film, which individually resemble a space blanket. The metallisation, consisting of silver, takes on a golden colour at a thickness of a few atomic layers. The metal layer of an MLI functions as a mirror, the plastic layer as a thermal insulator. The thermal insulation between the reflective layers is significantly

improved by coarsely meshed intermediate layers of silk or plastic. MLI foils protect satellites from cooling ill. Climate.14.1, p. 45 by reflecting heat back into them; they are also used to encourage the even distribution of heat and reflect external radiation to prevent heat gain.[19]

17
See Zimmermann (2005), 7th International Vacuum Insulation Symposium Empa. Cremers (2007), Vakuum-Dämmsysteme.
18
See Schmidt (1995), TTI in Architecture.
19
See Spinoff (1992), Reflective Insulation.

2.3 Thermoactive building systems TABS

The general functional principle of thermoactive building systems (TABS)[20] represents a further possibility for the design of climate-regulating surfaces for cooling and heating buildings. CLIMATE Technical Background 3, p.127 Such building elements are, for the most part, surface building components (wall, ceiling and floor plate) made of concrete, which incorporate pipe systems carrying (usually) water. ill. Climate.18.1, p.55, ill. Climate.18.2, p.55 Heat can either be transferred to (or removed from) the building component, which is slow to store heat, depending on the temperature of the water flowing within the piping system. The surface temperature of the building component, which can be adjusted in this way, is actively related to the room temperature, in terms of control. If the room temperature is higher, the TAB has a cooling effect; if it is lower, it functions as heating. The surfaces of the TAB must be in direct contact with the room air; cladding and hangings impair its functioning. There is a close relationship to the input of solar radiation, which is transformed into heat by the TAB, and thus to the geometry and orientation of the building in general and to the façade in particular (window-to-façade ratio, light guidance, shading). As a rule, the input from solar radiation must be limited, owing to the high heat loads produced and the limited cooling capacity of the activated building components. This applies especially to buildings in which many people are present for long periods of time, or in which a lot of heat-emitting technical equipment is used. TABs are sometimes seen as an alternative to air conditioning systems. The system variants include pure building component cooling by TABs in combination with conventional heating and ventilation systems, supplementary systems, and TABs used as the sole heating and cooling system in combination with mechanical ventilation.

3 Skin

The potential of 'skin' as a design concept can be illustrated graphically with reference to a series of prototypical studies following the line of logic developed in the preceding section.

[20] The acronym TABS is intended to cover related terms such as active surface system, component cooling, concrete core activation and underfloor heating. As a criterion for the further subdivision of TABS, Bine (2007) names the position of the pipes within the component, such as their position within the screed of underfloor heating systems. See Bine (2007), Thermoactive Building Systems.

The first of these approaches (fundamentally the most extreme) involves the direct realisation of the envelope as a synthetic,

quasi biological skin. This finds expression in the idea of biots SURFACES Discourse, p. 62, based on the technical ideal of *Tissue Engineering*,[21] in the *Construction In Vivo* approach

ill. Nano.03.3, p. 29; NANO Discourse 4, p. 72; Nano.03, p. 163 and in the concept of neoplasmatic design described above. ill. Climate.09.1, p. 17; Climate.09, p. 176

A second derivative of the skin analogy views it as a membrane or layer permeated with vessels, which can adjust its 'thermal conductivity' by altering the circulation conditions and regulating the fluid balance via the skin's pores. The technical interpretation of this

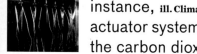

basic principle can be found in TABS. It is expressed in the *Smaq* bath project, ill. Climate.02.1, p. 16; Climate.02, p. 161 the most conspicuous component of which is a surface-maximising network of rubber hoses through which water flows. In its entirety, the bath forms its own miniature atmospheric system.

A third variation on the skin analogy involves deductive approaches that refer to the skin as a multifunctional protective envelope built up of layers (epidermis, dermis, subcutaneous tissue, connective and adipose tissue). This approach correlates most closely with the concept of construction layers in building physics. Various studies have been undertaken to investigate these functional layers experimentally. The *Living Glass* prototypical air control system, for

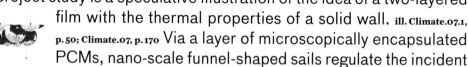

instance, ill. Climate.06.1, p. 28; Climate.06, p. 169 is based on a sensor-actuator system INFORMATION Technical Background 2.1, p. 146 that measures the carbon dioxide content of the room air and, when limit values are reached, deforms the slit polyacrylic glass by means of micromotors, so regulating the inflow of fresh air. The *Massive Skin* project study is a speculative illustration of the idea of a two-layered

film with the thermal properties of a solid wall. ill. Climate.07.1, p. 50; Climate.07, p. 170 Via a layer of microscopically encapsulated PCMs, nano-scale funnel-shaped sails regulate the incident solar radiation according to the MEMS principle NANO Technical Background 4, p. 81; INFORMATION Technical Background 2.1, p. 146 and so increase the efficiency of the heat reservoir. They also control the radiating properties of the foil, which can emit heat either inwards or outwards.

21
See also Del Campo and Manninger (2008), Speculations on Tissue Engineering and Architecture.

A variant of the fourth derivative, 'skin and bones', can be found in the bioconstructivist design of the *Batwing* by *Emergent*, in which the 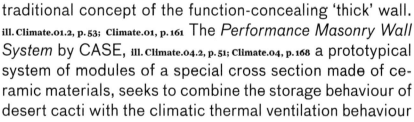 envelope and supporting structure, together with service engineering supply systems, are formed as an exoskeleton **ill. Climate.03.2, p. 35; Climate.03, p. 161** modelled on that of insects.

4 Capsule

With the ideal of the passive house, a variant of the capsule principle has been elevated to the status of a standard in which ambitious energy-saving specifications are met mostly by simplifying certain developments of existing technical principles and solutions. The result, which is not free of contradictions, involves an airtight insulated envelope that minimises exchange while, in an ideal green way, making contact with the outside world via ventilation systems (fresh air filters).[22] In this situation, the climate design of capsules involves a search for envelope concepts of appropriate complexity that transcend the simple hermetic principle. The installation *A Styrofoam Lover with (E)Motions of Concrete* explores the possibilities of generating a positive alternative from current methods of thermal renovation, using thick layers of polystyrene panels in combination with the traditional concept of the function-concealing 'thick' wall. **ill. Climate.01.2, p. 53; Climate.01, p. 161** The *Performance Masonry Wall System* by CASE, **ill. Climate.04.2, p. 51; Climate.04, p. 168** a prototypical system of modules of a special cross section made of ceramic materials, seeks to combine the storage behaviour of desert cacti with the climatic thermal ventilation behaviour of termite mounds. Equally illuminating are the solutions developed in detail by Jan Cremer, inspired by lightweight construction, for the construction of non-load-bearing exterior wall systems with integrated vacuum insulation systems. **ill. Climate.08.2, p. 59; ill. Climate.08, p. 172** Finally, in House R129 **ill. Surfaces.08.2, p. 12; Surfaces.08, p. 174** the famous concept of the polyvalent wall, which its inventor Mike Davies describes as a 'wall for all seasons', is brought together with the idea of the Pillow nomadic studio developed by the alternative Ant Farm collective. Davies describes in detail the multi-layered structure of a millimetre-thick envelope to generate power and heat,[23] which in its formal, speculative structure bears striking similarities to the layer principle of modern

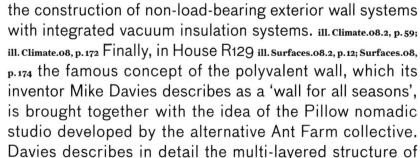

22 See Sommer (2008), Passivhäuser.

23 See Davies (1990), A Wall for all Seasons.

OLEDs. LIGHT Technical Background 4.2, p. 113 Conceived in 1981, it remains a valid vision—and one that we have come significantly closer to realising, thanks to the possibilities offered by nanotechnical thin-layer methods NANO Technical Background 3, p. 75 for creating energy-generating and light-generating surfaces ENERGY Technical Background 1, p. 89; LIGHT Technical Background 4, p. 112 and by sensor technology, INFORMATION Technical Background 2, p. 144 as well as by modern composite material systems based on glass or and plastics. SURFACES Discourse, p. 66 It is planned to use the aforementioned technologies in House R129. The similarity of the renderings of R129 to the photographically documented pneumatic envelope *Pillow* by *Ant Farm*, dating from the 1970s, highlights the link between the high-technology concept and the architectural redefinitions of a group committed to social countermodels: *'Ant Farm remained engaged with their historical moment, seeking political and aesthetic potentials inherent within new technologies.'*[24]

24
See Scott (2007), Architecture or Techno-utopia, p. 180.

INFORMATION Discourse

1 Information fora

Information is always concerned with space, in the sense that its main purpose lies in the connection of areas and locations that are separate from each other in terms of space or time. It extends ways of handling distances in time and theoretically promotes the linkage of disparate contexts to the point of their synchronisation. The idea of information is closely associated with communication, and although discussions may be dominated by the Internet at present, they also call to mind a considerable number of infrastructural (communicative) relations based on the logic of the surfaces developed here, whether functional, energy- and light-generating, or climate-regulating ones. The multi-facetted and powerful term 'information' plays a role in many cultural (and also technical) issues that have repeatedly been described as systems or networks. Although no standard definitions exist, (only context-related ones) variations of the simple sender-receiver model form the axiomatic basis of analytical and activity-oriented systems. Information in an everyday sense of the word means 'the facts provided', which is a 'communication' as it were. In terms of communications engineering, information is the spatial or chronological sequence of physical signals that occur with specific probabilities or frequencies and which make up a message, eliciting a thinking process in the recipient, resulting in a reaction, which turns into information again.

In the field of architecture and design, information generally adopts one of three pragmatic forms. Active[1] information-conveying surfaces present images and symbols using written characters, signs, display monitors and projections, or allow direct (targeted, intuitive or playful) utilisation of information via control systems. They supplement, complete or superimpose objects and architectural structures to the point of forming complex relationships in the form, for example, of guidance systems, media façades, or symbiotic medial leisure and working environments. **ill. Information.10.2, p. 29;**

1
A currently popular, yet confusing, formulation of the model is 'interactivity'. Technology-based interactive systems can hardly be found at this stage, these being at best under development. They are normally branched reactive systems, the programmed complexity of which is perceived to be so true-to-life that they are called 'interactive'. Interactivity touches on artificial intelligence issues. One branch of informatics research is concerned with the design of intelligent networks as semantic networks, with which machines are supposed to be made able to interpret information ('understand').
See Gold (1998), Der Mensch in der Perspektive der Kognitionswissenschaften. Wiener (1990), Probleme künstlicher Intelligenz. Haque (2006), Arquitetura, Interação e Sistemas.

Information.10, p. 176 Essential for understanding this development is the continually progressing miniaturisation of technology, reaching out into space more and more in the form of nano- and microengineering and allowing the creation of *intelligent environments*. A second form involves systems, networks and surfaces, from simple line systems to inductive or wireless power and data networks.

ill. Information.13.1, p. 14 Based on another assumption, according to which information is bound to physical carrier media, these form the medial environment for the transmission and storage of information. Information environments include domestic technical lines and control systems for water, heat, light and air. From a technical point of view, quantities such as circulating water or thermal energy cannot however be directly classified as information, even though this might be rather attractive for an overall consideration of system design. Strictly speaking, these line systems, including the associated energy- and light-generating or climate-regulating surfaces, become part of the information environment in the form of digital data obtained via measurement,

control and regulation units. **ill. Nano.16.1, p. 59;** INFORMATION Technical Background 2.1, p. 146 A third form includes the methods of coding information developed in the fields of design, architecture and urban development over long periods of time, representing the contents of professional education in these disciplines today. This includes elementary knowledge of symbols, colour, form, composition, rhythm and space, as well as of human behaviour and cultural characteristics. There is a reason for the recent gain in the importance of interdisciplinary strategies that purposely select an architectural, spatial approach to information design. These can be traced back to considerations by the computer experts Hiroshi Ishii and Brygg Ullmer who discussed 'new architectonic spaces' back in 1997, in which every surface, including walls, ceilings, windows, doors and desks, is included as a potentially information-active surface, allowing people to exert real and virtual influence on that room and on other rooms. According to Ishii and Ullmer, culture-specific architectural elements and settings can be unique starting points for information design.

William Gibson, Neuromancer, p. 68

He closed his eyes. Round the rigid face of the power stud. And in the bloodlit dark behind his eyes, silver phosphenes boiling in from the edge of space, hypnagogic images jerking past like film compiled from random frames. Symbols, figures, faces, a blurred, fragmented mandala of visual information. Please, he prayed, *now*— A gray disk, the color of Chiba sky. *Now*—

Ullmer illustrates this with the 'genkan', a kind of entrance area in Japanese houses, where shoes are taken off and the 'dirt' of the outside world is left behind—in a real and a metaphorical sense. Every Japanese person practices this ritual. In the context of Japanese culture, this would lend itself particularly well to information design, establishing an analogy between a physical and virtual 'genkan', transferring a ritual associated with a real room to a corresponding digital area.[2]

2 Three spaces

Until recently, infrastructures were considered to dictate the shape of architectural and urban design, but the powers attributed to the modern communication system Internet are of an almost mythical quality. The Director of the McLuhan Program in Culture and Technology at the University of Toronto, Derrick de Kerckhove, describes the character of the *Internet* and our role as witnesses to history in powerful words. With the exponential force of its own big bang (the invention of electricity), says de Kerckhove, *cyberspace* is exploding into existence right before our eyes.[3] Using the big bang theory that is supposed to explain how outer space once came to exist, de Kerckhove establishes a triad relating the cultural consequences of communication technology to architectural space. The rapidly spreading, basically technical, physical communication networks and the associated emanations of computer technology become an independent, virtual sphere, existing parallel to physically real and mental space (the 'world in our minds').[4] This scenario calls to mind many facets of the most important technical development of our time, changing the world as we know it. It describes both the apprehension, as well as the fascination, of the apparently inevitable and opens up specific options for dealing with the new conditions, with the claim of an eventual co-existence of the different categories of *space* (similar to Nordmann in the previous case of *nanospace*). NANO Discourse 1, p. 68 Following de Kerckhove's theory that the predominant cultural techniques of information-processing influence the perception of and the relation to space in a direct and simple manner, information design almost inevitably also becomes a task falling within the scope of architecture.[5] Like Ishii, de Kerckhove also considers architecture to have the capacity to support the physical and mental linkage of body and mind in many people.[6] His approach regards the prevailing information culture of a society as an important factor influencing that society's relationship to architecture, which is almost the opposite of Ishii's point of view. This offers designers

2
It would be conceivable, for example, to switch off electronic devices and thereby enter a digital rest zone. See Ullmer (2002), Tangible Interfaces, p. 212. In the same way, structural design elements such as handrails, posts, window and door frames could double up as linear display and control surfaces. Ishii and Ullmer also describe a correspondence between digital and spatial organisation, with the division of spatial units using intelligent room dividers representing digital segments, while the shelves and other furniture become three-dimensional settings for the organisation and conveyance of analogue and digital information. See Lipschitz (2004), Ubiquitious Computing.

3
See De Kerckhove (2001), The Architecture of Intelligence.

4
De Kerckhove (2001), The Architecture of Intelligence, p. 12.

5
"The connection between the Greek alphabetic literacy and city grids is neither fortuitous nor accidental, but direct. The use of letters [...] introduced a new relationship to space among the cultures that practised it. [...] space became objective reality. [...] We have to assume that Hippodamus was an avid reader."
De Kerckhove (2001), The Architecture of Intelligence, pp. 8–10.

6
"Architecture could certainly be the term that we need, a common basis for research and coordination of the three spaces." De Kerckhove (2001), The Architecture of Intelligence, p. 18.

a further (very individual and rewarding) approach to this subject. It is interesting in this respect to note that the Latin word *informare* can be translated to mean to *shape or fashion*. In a very basic sort of way, a designed room is therefore also an informed room (and vice versa). The need to shape the expanding information space actively (or conversely 'spatialise' information) is related to the degree of inter-relationship between space and information.

Based on a scenario in which material networks result in virtual spaces as described above, it can be said that each individual is surrounded by latent information-active surfaces. These can be envisaged as active envelope systems, in the sense of bubbles that can develop, divide or combine to form meta-systems. The information potential of each sphere depends on its scope and the size of the overall system of which it is a part. This simple model allows the designability of information to be represented as the design of the basic technical, material characteristics of surfaces and networks dependent on their actual distance to the individual, i.e. from inside to outside. This appears logical in view of the fact that information requires media for its creation, transmission and storage. The envelope model is also consistent with regard to the dimension-based logic followed in this book (nano, micro, macro, cosmos).

If the technical aspect is considered again at this point, it becomes evident that the many approaches to designing information envelopes can be categorised according to a few key terms and fundamental technologies and, ultimately, the categories *surface (interface)* and *network*. The complexities described above can therefore be summarised by the following expression: *interface* and *network engineering* (described in the final section) are used to design and construct information envelopes. The conceptual classifications

- body-near information-active surfaces
- intelligent environments
- intelligent building envelopes
- location-related information networks

John Clute, Appleseed, p. 87

From the shadowy fluted ceiling dangled, like the vertebrae of a never-ending story, long figurative dramas in azulejaria porcelain. The grouting between each glowing blue tile leaked gold enamelling deep into the dramas: tales of intolerable eros typical of Human Earth, accomplished fingers caressing piccolos and bare breasts. The mask resident within the stories stared outward through moist beeeye-dense between molten grouts of gold.

are a useful means of differentiation in the description of information envelopes. Using these in conjunction with the technical categories permits the theoretical discussion and linkage of almost all of the tasks involved in information design, at dimensions ranging from portable accessories to large-scale building structures and beyond. The scope of the discussion can be illustrated by two examples. In the search for solutions for so-called *ambient displays*, prototypical solutions from three of the cited information spheres include cyber glasses, a transparent screen and a media façade. These can be compared in terms of content and technology (LED, OLED, holographic systems, projections).[7] LIGHT Technical Background 2, p.107 The model of corresponding information envelopes, however, also makes the formulation of project ideas easier. It is, for instance, conceivable to influence the reaction of the building envelope (heating, ventilation) via constant measurement of body temperature by means of intelligent clothing. **ill. Information.03.1, p. 42; Information.03, p. 169;** CLIMATE Discourse 2, p.117 Some refinement of the initial model allows the modes of function and the steps necessary for realising it to be described precisely and quickly.

3 Information spheres and envelopes

The innermost information sphere of body-near information-active surfaces comprises the 'strange cavity' of the head[8] and the human senses. The systems that can be outlined in this context include systems directly in contact with the body, or even in symbiosis with the body, such as clothing with sensors measuring skin biodata, or subcutaneously implanted sensors, body-near actuators, smart contact lenses, **ill. Information.19.1, p. 23** glasses, data gloves and other forms of intelligent clothing fitted with micro- and nano-engineering based devices. The aim of this so-called s*mart clothing* or *wearable computing* technology is to be small and light enough not to bother the wearer. It opens up ways of transferring, as it were, modern conventional technical aids, such as mobile phones or music players, to the body and ways of turning prosthetic solutions into permanent extensions of human perception and information processing capacities. Monitoring systems for long-term screening as part of medical preventive care, or for emergencies, could also be feasible. A body-near information envelope is a hermaphrodite sort of fabric composed of nano- and microsized interfaces and networks.[9]

The next group includes the surrounding space and the *objects* contained therein, constituting the genuine field of interface design. The important concepts of *Graphic User Interface (GUI)* and *Tangible User Interface (TUI)*, normally used in combination for

7
In a nutshell: in this case the concept is easily scaleable, but the technical solutions are not.

8
Spoken to Michel Foucault, See Foucault (1966), Der utopische Körper.

9
An overview of the potential of intelligent clothing is provided in Seymour (2009), Fashionable Technology.

controlling and operating a now enormous number of devices and technical systems, were established in this field first. INFORMATION Technical Background 2.2, p. 150 Computers and mobile phones have, in the meantime, become everyday objects. Theoretically, however, every domestic technology control mechanism (switch, valve, door handle, lock) could be simulated or replaced by a new operation logic using GUI and TUI and the associated microelectronics and specialised (also wireless) subsystems, via

small touchscreens for example.[10] ill. Information.15.1, p. 20; INFORMATION Technical Background 1.2, p. 141 Parallel to the trend of increasing miniaturisation of technology and the spread of wireless networks, many new forms of handling information are being developed at present, which also aim to include the actual environment as a physical movement space and collective action space. INFORMATION Technical Background 1.3, p. 144 This development has repeatedly also been explained in terms of the limitations of GUI systems. Ishii differentiates very clearly between graphic and tactile forms of representation of digital information elements or 'bits'. While the two-dimensional *painted bits* of GUI link the handling of information almost exclusively to the sense of vision, leading to a passive physical behaviour, multi-dimensional tangible bits are intended to allow inclusion of all the other senses and activation of the body's motor system.[11] In this manner, they provide access to a whole series of new approaches based on spatial and everyday experiences, and therefore inherently more intuitive. These approaches are unified by the presumption that physical activity 'supplies us simultaneously with information about the world surrounding us and about ourselves'. Very broad concepts such the embodiment concept assume that the brain 'as organ of the mind' cannot work intelligently without being embedded in the environment via an active body.[12]

As a genuine micro-level, the intelligent environment sphere is probably the area that has been discussed in the greatest detail up to now.[13] INFORMATION Technical Background 1, p. 140 Numerous terms and concepts (including *Ambient Intelligence, Ubiquitous Computing, Pervasive Computing, Internet of Things*) are used to describe intelligent environments.[14] Despite the many extensive theoretical and precise conceptual descriptions,[15] there are very few applications in existence beyond the prototype stage, apart

from the touchscreen and position-sensitive controllers. ill. Information.27.1, p. 42; INFORMATION Technical Background 2.1, p. 146 Within information technology, embodiment

10
See Flusser (1994), Gesten.
11
Bill Moggridge interview with Hiroshi Ishii. Moggridge (2006), Designing Interactions, p. 513.
12
See Form+Zweck 22 (2008), Tangibility of the Digital, p. 8.
13
For a definition of embodiment, see Maja Storch et al., Embodiment, Bern 2006, p. 15. Also informative in this regard are Zeynep Çelik's studies on the historical development of the term kinaesthetics: 'According to Hermann von Helmholtz (1821 – 1894) [...] the functioning of muscles was identical to the operations of logic [...] This kind of knowledge, Kennen, [...] was associated with the exercising of the muscles. It differed from the conventional kind of knowledge, Wissen, which was based on cognition and language.' Çelik (2006), Kinaesthesia.
14
According to the computer scientist Friedemann Mattern at the Institute for Pervasive Computing, ETH Zurich, the terms can be allocated to different scientific or practical communities, but essentially describe the same thing: Computers are becoming smaller and smaller, eventually being taken up by the environment and everyday objects—making the environment 'smart' and supporting human beings in an unobtrusive way. See Asut Bulletin 4 (2007), Interview with F. Mattern.
15
See Hornecker and Buur (2006), Getting a Grip on Tangible Interaction.

can be related to robotics, for example, and considered as the missing component for functioning artificial intelligence systems *(embedded artificial intelligence)*. Other solutions being worked on in this field mainly involve the further technical development of combinations of TUI and GUI, in which the visual aspect continues to play an important role. Design and architecture-related approaches are primarily based on haptics. Examples of this include mobile surfaces that operate using actuators and microengineering, and kinetic objects that mainly rely on specially developed information representation systems.

The term 'intelligent envelope' refers to the information sphere of spatial structures and buildings. Although much of what has been mentioned above in relation to the sphere of surrounding space and the size of objects can be applied to this area, the dimensions of room and building envelopes are inevitably larger and therefore represent a substantial jump in scale from a technical point of view. If the miniaturisation of technology is a trend of immanent orientation to spatial relationships, scaling it up to wall formats requires a skilled interpretation of the given technol-

 ogy, **ill. Information.08.2, p. 40; Information.08, p. 174** or its further development under different premises. The technical solutions permitted by an object-related touchscreen of about 3×5 cm are different to those permitted by one the size of a wall.[16]

 ill. Information.20.1, p. 23 The two major ideas determining the design of intelligent envelopes are, firstly, the technically highly integrated wall-format solution, i.e. the ideal of 'wallpaper' as discreet, simple and planar installations for transmitting information. **ill. Surfaces.16.1, p. 46** The second involves the major theoretical idea of 'skin' already presented in the Climate section, CLIMATE Discourse 2, p. 117 and includes the aspects of Nano, Energy and Light for complex information systems. Both can theoretically be realised either directly, using the material, or novel technical surfaces, or else through a combination of materials, such as wall systems composed of segments and functional layers. NANO Discourse 2, p. 69; CLIMATE Technical Background 2, p. 122 A third approach is the development of intelligent room structures via sensor, control and management

John Clute, Appleseed, p. 12

Blank me, he subvocalised into conclaved space, turning away from the humming cube. [...] Through his data gloves he stroked a tile mask, which had responded to his slight distress. The tile made a blank purring sound—no AI was parking within its tiny brain—and returned to its place beside its companions, on the curved walls of control centre.

16
See **Comparing touchscreen technologies** (2009), Also Saffer (2009), **Designing Gestural Interfaces**.

technologies, which have already been discussed. These in turn provide the circular argument leading to microengineering and new, small-format, sensor-actuator technology, **fig. Sensor–actuator p. 150** basically transforming every unspecific surface into an intelligent surface.

ill. Information.11.2, p. 19; Information.11, p. 178 New developments in this area allow expert systems, low-tech and individual solutions to be designed. INFORMATION Technical Background 2.2, p. 150 As applied to interior spaces, an envelope is perceived as a service system for the inhabitants, while an orientation to the exterior allows information surfaces to be considered as media façades reaching, for example, into urban environments. LIGHT Discourse 1, p. 101

The final group to be described is the one referred to as location-related information networks. This group represents, so to speak, the meta-level of all the information envelopes described earlier. It is based on sensor engineering. One trend involves the development

of wireless sensor networks, called *smart dust*. **ill. Nano.16.1, p. 59;** INFORMATION Technical Background 2.1, p. 146 In addition to specific purpose-made constructions, there is increasing development of economical, standardised structures that can be implemented in a context-related manner using programming. Such sensor kits exist for all of the three information spheres described above.[17]

ill. Information.33.1, p. 55; INFORMATION Technical Background 3, p. 155 Examples of them include supply networks with integrated sensor technology, as well as individually designed communication networks reaching into local public spaces and even into global networks, the material condition of which we only notice in the rare event of their failure.[18]

ill. Information.18.1, p. 22 If cameras and satellites are also included as image-producing sensors, then the list of possible (and already realised) location- or context-related information networks influencing our

William Gibson, Neuromancer, p. 16

The brown laminate of the tabletop was dull with a patina of tiny scratches. With the dex mounting through his spine he saw the countless random impacts required to create a surface like that. The Jarre was decorated in a dated, nameless style from the previous century, an uneasy blend of Japanese traditional and pale Milanese plastics, but everything seemed to wear a subtle film, as though the bad nerves of a million customers had somehow attacked the mirrors and the once glossy plastics, leaving each surface fogged with something that could never be wiped away.

[17] Examples for the given order are *LilyPads, RFID chips* and so-called *motes*.

[18] See Submarine cable disruption (2008), http://en.wikipedia.org/wiki/2008_submarine_cable_disruption.

everyday lives basically starts at nano- and micro-level (e.g. medical measurement of vital functions) and continues through macro-space (e.g. vibration measurements on buildings) to end in the cosmos (e.g. Global Information System GIS, CLIMATE Discourse 2, p. 117). The efficiency of such technology gives rise to the necessity of open systems. INFORMATION Technical Background 2, p. 144

INFORMATION Technical Background

Interface technologies

Information-active surfaces[1] or *interfaces* are transmission points or contact surfaces between at least two areas, generally tantamount to a transformation of information. On an elementary level, this is represented by the relationship between man and machine.[2] The development of interface design as a discipline has been influenced by the technology available. A currently observable trend is the dissolution of machine intelligence into space, paraphrased as 'the disappearance of the computer',[3] which is attributable to the miniaturisation of technology in combination with the emergence of wireless networks. This development makes the design of intelligent surfaces more flexible. Following de Kerckhove's thinking, this permits a greater diversity of ways of transmitting information, which in turn promotes the sought-after overlap of the three spaces discussed in the preceding section of this book. This is why the design of bordering surfaces should logically start by interweaving architectural and technical know-how with visual communication. The radical nature

of projects such as the *Media House Project* ill. Information.05.2, p. 58; Information.05, p. 170 is not evident so much in the implanted technology (which will probably be available to us relatively soon) as in the consistency with which the house is conceived as a built information envelope.[4] Interface design concepts can be assigned to one of three basic categories: *Ambient Displays,*

1
The fact that location-related events and technical processes are coded as virtual digital data that can also be reproduced elsewhere and be manipulated, is significant for an understanding of information-active surfaces and networks. Although the resulting consequences cannot be discussed in detail here, they are fairly evident.

2
Relevant research refers to Man-Machine Systems (MMS) or Human Computer Interface (HCI) design. The most far-reaching formulation of MMS is probably the expression cyborg (cybernetic organism) coined in 1960, which has been interpreted in many different ways.
See Clynes und Kline (1960), Cyborgs and Space. Also: Hables-Gray (1995), The Cyborg Handbook.

3
Weiser (1991), The Computer for the Twenty-First Century.

4
"The House is the computer. The structure is the network." See Guallarte (2005), Media House Project.

Tangible User Interfaces and *Augmented Reality*. The scope of these terms is generally considered to cover the majority of current ubiquitous computing developments. The concepts need to be seen in the context of advancing network technologies, particularly sensor and radio chip technology, with which synergies are increasingly becoming apparent.

1.1 Ambient displays

The designation *Ambient Displays* (AD) is used to define a broader view of display. The term tends to describe inconspicuous and well-integrated displays that are not immediately recognisable as what they are: screens for providing constant, situation-related, visible and accessible information. A discussion of ADs necessarily includes a consideration of new technologies involving flexible, transparent displays and power-saving technologies such as OLED technology.

LIGHT Technical Background 4.2, p. 113 Examples such as the *Interactive Tablecloth,* which conveys information by controlled changes of colours of the woven multilayer fabric, ill. Surfaces.19.2, p. 56 the mechanical semitone display *Aperture,* ill. Information.32.2, p. 50 or the *Echologue-Display* ill. Information.02.1, p. 31; Information.02, p. 165 with its elegant simplicity, clearly demonstrate that AD design is always the result of an overall consideration of context, technology and information content, and that it can also be achieved using *low tech*.

The list should include a project following up the e-paper[5] idea, flicflex, ill. Information.22.2, p. 24 a design study exploring the use of ADs as intuitive *Tangible User Interfaces*. In future, the built environment will be permeated by ADs in the form of particularly large ill. Light.17.1, p. 46 and particularly small ill. Information.34.2, p. 55 smart surfaces.

[5] E-paper is basically intended to combine the typical usage of paper with that of electronic displays. This is achieved by using electrically conductive plastics containing tiny spheres in which electronic ink (e-ink) pigments react to voltage. Some major e-ink manufacturers supply prototype kits for experimentation. Electro-wetting involves liquids (microfluids) making up innumerable tiny drop-shaped pixels, the surface tension of which is influenced minimally by electric currents for displaying information. See Hayes and Feenstra (2002), Electrowetting.

1.2 Tangible user interfaces

The computer mouse is an object that most of us use every day, which in itself gives us a direct idea of the character and functions of Tangible User Interfaces. TUIs can be described as physical surfaces that can be touched, and which contain the mechanisms for the active control of digital information. The physically perceptible states of TUIs represent key states of the associated digital system and allow the targeted generation of control information within the scope of rules that can be perceived via the senses. TUIs should be distinguished from non-tangible interfaces (speech or gesture-controlled). Further development, however, aims at system combinations involving *multimodal interaction*[6] and *whole body interaction*. ill. Information.29.1, p. 44 In the meantime, *interaction design*[7] describes so many different approaches to TUI, including experimental ones, that the course of development outlined by the pioneers Ishii and Ullmer is sometimes characterised as a 'data-centred view'.[8]

Any discussion of TUIs should include touchscreen technology, for which a whole series of technical solutions has been developed by the industry: *'Tap is the new Click.'*[9] There are, for instance, the more economical analog-resistive systems, the capacitive systems often used in mobile phones, and optical systems that employ an array of infrared LEDs in a glass or plastic panel, instead of an electrical resistance or field. The LEDs transmit a pattern across the narrow side of the panel which is detected by sensors located on the opposite side. Touching the surface interrupts the path of projection of the beams, with certain light beams 'not reaching the detectors'. The position of the finger can therefore be registered as an interference, using the projection grid. fig. Touchscreen, p. 143 Identification of the position on the display surface is linked to a GUI display. The FTIR technology developed by Jeff Han is a version of this principle that is both robust and efficient.[10] It allows the development of intuitively usable, large-format touchscreens. ill. Information.20.1, p. 23 Besides these

6
Development of multimodal control systems is currently concentrated on mobile phone applications. The potentials of space-related multimodal interaction are demonstrated by the work of Mignonneau (2003), Poesie des Programmierens.

7
See Moggridge (2007), Designing Interactions. For an introduction to the subject presenting an up-to-date picture of the situation that is well worth reading.
An introduction to the subject that reflects current viewpoints is given by Lowgren (2009), Interaction Design.

8
Ullmer and Ishii (2001), Emerging Frameworks for Tangible User Interfaces. An update of this original work is discussed by Eva Hornecker and Jacob Buur. The four categories of Tangible Manipulation, Spatial Interaction, Embodied Facilitation and Expressive Representation are developed for the differentiation of existing and future TUIs. See Hornecker and Buur (2006), Getting a Grip on Tangible Interaction.

9
Saffer (2008), Designing Gestural Interfaces, p. 3.
Gestural control is becoming more important in a touchscreen context. For a general explanation of gesture see Flusser (1997), Gesten.

10
Han (2005), Low-Cost Multi-Touch Sensing.

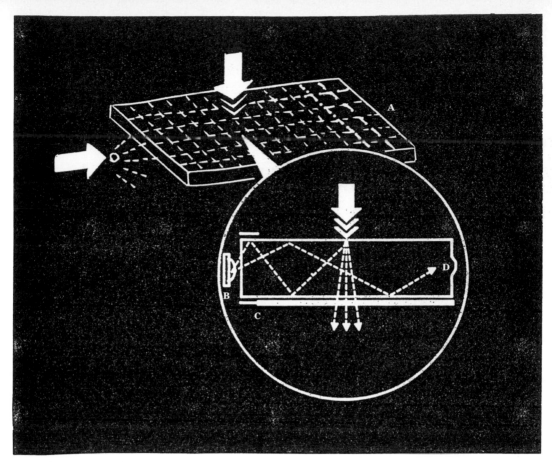

fig. Touch screen
A = acrylic glass panel, B = infra-red light source, C = diffuser for projection, D = infra-red sensor

multimedia-oriented applications, there are comparatively few concepts that manage without image projection at the moment. Although these generally appear rather more experimental at first, they are all the more interesting, because they are characterised by a reduced complexity, which could lead towards the design of pseudo-architectural or architecture-specific surfaces that are sensitive to touch.

The *GranulatSynthese Interface* allows the intuitive control of a light and sound installation by manually moving and accumulating granules. Similar at first sight, but conceptually more radical, is the approach of *New Sensual Interfaces*, ill. Information.06.1, p. 43; Information.06, p. 172 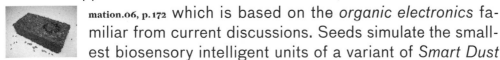 which is based on the *organic electronics* familiar from current discussions. Seeds simulate the smallest biosensory intelligent units of a variant of *Smart Dust* that can be used to create intuitive interfaces by development from personal patterns of thinking and acting, as well as completely new forms of interaction with digital data.

1.3 Augmented reality

Augmented Reality is a technology intended to enrich the real world with computer-generated set pieces of context-related information for acoustic, visual or tactile perception in real time, thereby extending sensory capacities. These are not to be confused with the total representation of artificial worlds as in *Virtual Reality*. A typical AR application would be to superimpose the optical perception of the real world with congruent visual information, supplied to the field of vision dynamically, via projections or transparent displays, and continuously synchronised with the movement of the eyes, head and other parts of the body linked to the sensory system. fig. Augmented Realities, p. 145 An interesting version of this is the production of large-format spatial landscapes with true-to-contour computer-aided projection

systems, as used in the *Polygon Playground*. ill. Information.21.1, p. 24 This manages without any cumbersome cyberglasses or data gloves and is spontaneously accessible. The continual miniaturisation of technical hardware will promote the spread of AR applications, while their implementation in real world contexts will be facilitated by mini-sensors, pico-projectors, transparent displays and miniscule cameras. Open software platforms such as ARTToolKit[11] offer a relatively simple introduction to the subject, presenting a great variety of interesting experiments, many of which are currently based on using the cameras in mobile phones. The inherent potential of AR

for the development of creative processes is demonstrated by projects such as the *Augmented Studio* at the Bauhaus University of Weimar. ill. Information.10.2, p. 29; Information.10, p. 176

2 Network technologies

Networks are generally expected to perform a process with a quick reaction time, within a foreseeable period, which should be as short as possible (instantly and in real time). This applies to both wirebound and wireless networks, even though simple, low-transmission-rate solutions are purposely selected for certain applications such as sensor networks. They are also expected to be as inconspicuous and flexible as possible,

[11]
http://artoolkit.sourceforge.net/
The page claims to have registered over 160,000 downloads from the software library since 2004.

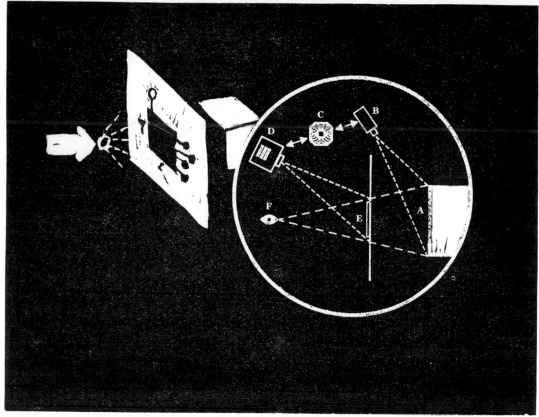

fig. Augmented Reality
A = real object, B = camera, C = processor, D = projector, E = level of overlap between A and D, F = observer

permitting good structural integration. Important factors additionally influencing network design include the purpose, the material and
structural composition[12] and the question of whether open or closed
systems are involved. This division leads to rather unfathomable issues, such as the economics, the protection of intellectual property
and how to control architectural spaces. Open systems are generally
considered to be more democratic than closed systems. The fact that
they can be interpreted collectively by users appears to result in their
quasi-spontaneous development. They normally represent a larger
variety of solutions, reflected by a great diversity in their forms of
appearance. Contexts play a decisive role
in a corresponding qualification of systems. A great number of graded, mixed
and juxtaposed varieties of networks have
evolved in the meantime, comparable to
the forms of social cohabitation arising

12
Evident with regard to software,
which has in the meantime become necessary for the operation of most
networks. Open networks require software that is open to interpretation
and vice versa. See also Stallmann
(2007), Why "Open Source" misses the
point of Free Software.

from urban development and architectural categories of public and private space. Empirical values relating to both technical and built networks (encompassing objects, architectural structures and cities) therefore exist. What will require renewed estimation are the synergies and conflict potentials arising from effects such as overlapping and increasing efficiency.

Considering networks and information-active surfaces as a whole, a division into simple *(low-tech)* and highly developed technology *(high-tech)* offers a dichotomy that is in turn usable in discussing design. *Low-tech* solutions, which generally also include a lower cost strategy, i.e. *low budget*, are normally robust, easy to operate and designed for rapid spread and participation. ill. Information.04.2, p. 15; Information.04, p. 170 The term *low-tech* does not, however, say anything about the intelligence of the technology behind the solution, and this occasionally leads to misunderstandings, because they do involve components that are ever more advanced technologically, but have in the meantime become easy to use, such as programmable microchips. INFORMATION Technical Background 3, p. 155 At first glance, in terms of the degree of technical complexity of a solution, *low-* and *high-tech* implicitly stand for the collective interpretability ill. Information.08.2, p. 40; Information.08, p. 174 of future actions, situations and architectural structures, as well as for their precise solution. ill. Surfaces.08.2, p. 12; Surfaces.08, p. 174

2.1 Sensors and actuators

A sensor,[13] also referred to as detector or probe, is a technical component that can register specific physical or chemical ambient conditions (e.g. temperature, moisture, pressure, sound, brightness or acceleration). These parameters are recorded by means of physical or chemical effects and transformed in the sensor to quantities that can be processed further (to electrical signals or digital data). The sensor output signals are processed by microprocessors and either displayed and evaluated via interfaces (e.g. screens) or passed on directly to control or regulating units, the actuators,[14] via amplifiers.

13
Sensors are elementary components of interfaces. See Igoe (2006), Sensor Interfaces, p. 161. They are discussed in the section about Network Technologies because their structure is mainly microtechnology-based and because sensor networks are becoming increasingly significant.

14
In robotics, an actuator is often called an effector. Effectors are used by robots to grab and work on objects, for example.

A system interacting with the environment normally functions on the basis of the interplay of

- sensors (senses of the structure)
- regulation and control system (brain of the structure)
- actuators (muscles of the structure).[15]

Sensor technology activated networks are similar to artificial nervous systems that act self-sufficiently depending on a previously defined condition. Intelligent sensor/actuator systems, the nanoscale to microscale varieties of which are also classified as NEMS or MEMS *(Nano- or Micro-Electro-Mechanical Systems)* and MOMS *(Micro-Opto-Mechanical Systems)* are currently being studied.

The huge number of sensors and associated areas of use can be ordered on the basis of a variety of principles. Sensors may, for example, be classified as analog or digital, and active (power-generating) or passive (relying on external power), as well as resistive (measuring change in electrical resistance), inductive (reacting only to metal) and capacitive (reacting to non-metals). A broader understanding can be gained by differentiating between special context-specific solutions and context-adapted versions of standard designs, as well as designs adapted by software programming. The way in which a sensor works depends on the condition that it is required to detect. One sensor commonly used in the building industry is the strain gauge. Its function is based on changes in the electrical resistance of the material used in the sensor, corresponding to changes in length caused by expansion and stress forces in building components.[16] Among other typical sensors are fire detectors and light barriers for controlling automatic doors. An increasingly important role is now played by accelerometers and the new microscopic gyrosensors.

ill. Information.27.1, p. 42 The latter can detect the dynamic status of an object (vibration behaviour, acceleration) and its orientation and position in a room by measuring the mass inertia.[17]

15
See Pawlowski (2006), Adaptive roof structures, p. 14. For further information about the basic model, please refer to: Teuffel (2004), Design of adaptive structures, p. 12.
16
Teuffel (2004), Design of adaptive structures, p. 13.
17
A typical orientation sensor is the gyroscope, invented in 1852, adaptations of which are also used for navigation (gyrocompass). The smallest currently available gyrosensors are only a few millimetres in size. Huge numbers of these are produced for applications including satellites, aircrafts, cars, mobile phones and video game controllers. Gyrosensors are considered to be a pioneering example of nanoscale machines. See also Tauschek (2007), Mikromaschinen.

Although apparently predestined for architectural and design applications, they have hardly been used in those areas up to now. Intensive studies are being conducted to explore potential medical sensing applications.[18]

Sensor arrays and sensor networks are designed when a number of sensors are required to work together. Particularly dense sensor arrangements are generally referred to as sensor arrays. Nanoscale arrays are implemented as neurochips in biomedicine, for example, where their interaction with living nerve cells is being studied. ill. Information.16.1, p.22 By distributing a large number of sensor nodes in the environment, wireless sensor networks (WSN) permit the detailed and extensive observation of real world phenomena. These sensor nodes, also known as motes, can be described as minicomputers (no larger than a shoe box) that are able to register environmental parameters via sensors. The information is then processed by processors, transmitted by wireless to nearby sensor nodes and finally transferred, node-by-node, to a central computer. Preliminary designs are already available as programmable standardised components. A sensor network should continue to function even if specific nodes fail owing, for example, to exhausted batteries. As for sensor arrays, the number of nodes and their precise context-related spatial distribution co-determine their functionality and the quality of the data that can be collected. Professionals also use the term 'network resolution' to describe this. Smart Dust[19] refers to the predicted construction of sensor networks consisting of nanoscale nodes capable of long-term function. Visionary descriptions of Smart Dust as clouds enveloping persons, objects, buildings and landscapes have extended to the critical discussion of sensor networks. This is because the idea of 'sensory' disposable microtechnology, ill. Nano.16.1, p.59 the size of a speck of dust, immediately conjures up a future with comprehensive and unnoticed surveillance of both private and public space.[20] On the positive side, there is of course enormous potential for the application of economical sensor nodes that can be attached and integrated as required—allowing any surface to be turned into a smart surface.

18
See Luinge and Veltink (2005), Measuring Orientation of Human Body. BodyNets Proceedings (2008), Also: Haque and Somlai-Fischer (2005), Low Tech Sensors and Actuators.
19
Warneke et al. (2001), Smart Dust.
20
Neal Stephenson's descriptions in his science fiction novel Diamond Age are well-known.

ill. Information.11.3, p. 19; Information.11, p. 178 Real world examples of applications for prototype sensor networks include monitoring buildings and outdoor areas,[21] as well as safeguarding the structural stability of traffic structures.[22]

Whereas sensors convert a physical quantity to electrical energy, actuators, being electromechanical components, do just the opposite: they convert electricity to sound, pressure, temperature, movement, light or torque. Examples of actuators include loudspeakers, lamps and motors, as well as pneumatic cylinders, piezo actuators, electrochemical actuators and ultrasonic motors. Measurement and control technology applications include opening and closing valves. Actuator materials with a smart character have emerged from the New Materials sector. Actuators based

on shape-memory ill. Climate.06.1, p. 28; Climate.06, p. 169 alloys and expansion elements are temperature-sensitive and used in thermostats, for example. Smart hydrogels are also used in chemostats, which automatically regulate pH, ion or material concentrations. Sensor/actuator systems are important in the design of adaptive roof structures,[23] mobile spatial structures, the kinetic skins of buildings[24] and intelligent clothing. ill. Information.03.1, p. 42; Informa-

tion.03, p. 169; fig. Sensor—Actuator, p. 150 They are also significant within the context of the e-home concepts described later. The work done by Usman Haque and Adam Somlai-Fischer represents a remarkable approach to the design of information-active spatial environments and building envelopes using sensor/actuator systems. Their ground-breaking projects are characterised by their prototypical and experimental nature, combined with open and par-

ticipative access for users. ill. Information.25.2, p. 40 Their handbook, *Low-Tech Sensors und Actuators for Artists and Architects*,[25] is an implicit documentation of this approach, offering a good introduction to the field described.

22
Dauberschmidt et al. (2008), Monitoring von Verkehrsbauten.
23
See Teuffel (2004), Entwerfen adaptiver Strukturen. Pawlowski (2006), Adaptive Dachtragwerke.
24
Michael A Fox offers an initial basis of kinetic architecture: "Designing such systems is not inventing, but appreciating and marshalling the technology that exists and extrapolating it to suit an architectural vision." Fox (2002), Beyond Kinetic.
25
Accessible at http://lowtech. propositions.org.uk/.

RFID

RFID stands for *Radio Frequency Identification* and describes a contactless technology for transmitting data by means of radio waves
beyond the field of vision. The basic RFID system infrastructure includes a transponder *(transmitter-responder)*, a transmitter-receiver
device (reader) and a background IT system (a database such as

fig. Sensor—Actuator
A = sensor, B = processor, C = actuator/muscle

the Internet). The key part of this technology is the transponder—a
tiny computer chip with an antenna. This is integrated in a carrier
object, such as a plastic card or an adhesive label (typically referred
 to as an RFID tag) attached to an object. ill. Information.18.1,
p. 22 The latest RFID transponders are the size of a grain
of rice and can be implanted. ill. Information.23.1, p. 28 The way
 in which the system works can be elucidated by considering the 'tricks' that it makes use of. It behaves like a small
radar system, except that the radio signal emitted by the
reader is not reflected passively by the transponder, but converted
into a manipulated answer signal (usually with a slightly modified
frequency) representing an individual number sequence. The RFID

transponder obtains the electrical energy required for this conversion from the transmission signal of the reader, the radio waves of which it can transform. Depending on the frequency range, signal strength and local environmental influences, data can be interrogated by the reader at a distance of several centimetres to several metres.[26] In its simplest form, the chip is a comparatively simple, passive, microelectronic component of limited intelligence, which develops minimal activity as soon as it enters the transmission range of the reader. As is already familiar to us from sensor networks, highly flexible and intelligent networks can be created using disposable components like this. The further development of RFID technology is currently concentrated on optimising system components. Active transponders, for instance, have become available: these possess a power supply of their own and therefore have a wider range and higher programmable intelligence, allowing them to store and transmit more extensive data packets. These applications do not require the readers to be connected to databases. Combinations of transponders with sensors are also being investigated, in which the transponders perform the function of transmitting the values recorded by the sensors.

The dynamically developing RFID technology is considered to be the key technology of ubiquitous computing[27] and is subject to controversial discussion. Although there are very high expectations of this technology in the field of logistics and commerce, in view of the prospect of potentially total control of the flow and production of goods, the influence of ubiquitous RFID networks on the privacy of individuals is a hotly disputed topic. RFID is, so to speak, synonymous with the *Internet of Things*[28] and therefore also increasingly perceived as a cultural phenomenon. This catchy phrase sums up the hypothesis dominating the discussion, according to which the ubiquity of objects coded with RFID chips will lead to development of an Internet-supported (and

26
RFID is in fact a comparatively old technology, the origins of which date back to the Second World War. Early forms were developed for differentiating whether an aircraft was friend or foe, for instance. A history of RFID technology is given by Rosol (2007), RFID. A short introduction to the fundamental technical principles is provided in: RFID Knowledge (2007). More detailed information is available in a study by Germany's Federal Office for Information Security (2004), Security Aspects and Prospective Applications of RFID Systems. Freely accessible in German and English on the BSI web site. See also Finkenzeller (2006), RFID-Handbuch [RFID Handbook].

27
Federal Office for Information Security (2004), Security Aspects and Prospective Applications of RFID-Systems, p. 19.

28
See Weiser (1991), The Computer for the Twenty-First Century, pp. 94–100. A worthwhile account relating to the term by Kranenburg (2008), The Internet of Things.

Internet-comparable), participative information and network culture in the real world. This is also represented by non-commercial, open hardware platforms such as *Arduino* ill. Information.14.1, p.18; INFORMATION Tech-

nical Background 2, p.144 and easy-to-use, economical RFID construction kits. Individual information environments, such as a mini-system for measuring the moisture of the soil in potted plants, which can then ask to be watered by means of a telephone call, can be created in this manner without requiring much previous knowledge of the subject. InHaus2 is a research project for optimising building site logistics and material flow, set up in Duisburg by the Fraunhofer Society (Fraunhofer Gesellschaft). During the building phase, transport containers for building materials and façade elements were equipped with RFID chips, which were scanned whenever a delivery vehicle passed a reader installed near the building site entrance gate.[29] Further InHaus2 tests included vacuum insulation panels CLIMATE Technical Background 2.2, p.124 monitored by RFID sensors, which report changes in the internal pressure that would lead to less efficient insulation. The system can be used to check the panels immediately after the critical installation phase. Another prototype set-up involved embedding passive RFID temperature sensor units in cast-in-place concrete ceilings. A simple concrete ceiling is converted to a temperature-sensitive, intelligent surface in this way, and becomes part of the building information system in respect of climate.[30]

2.3 Inductive networks and printable electronics

Inductive networks, printable electronics and piezoelectric systems ill. Energy.21.1, p.42; ENERGY Technical Background 3, p.97 are important technological approaches with enormous potential for designing smart surfaces. One of the two technologies currently under discussion, the radio frequency technology that also works over greater distances, has already been described. INFORMATION Technical Background 2.2, p.150 Inductive coupling makes use of coils that generate electromagnetic fields across a few centimetres, which can be received and transformed by electronic components fitted with transmission heads. The technology involved has been in use for quite some time, with the difference that it is now being developed further to achieve contactless (concurrent) transmission of electrical energy, information,

29
Meyer et al. (2008), Intelligent construction site logistics.

30
Wessel (2008), German Institute tests RFID in Construction.

or thermal energy. As with wireless networks, the system replaces cables and wires.[31] Inductive current conduction systems (similar to the energy-transmitting tabletop) for supplying storage batteries are being developed by a number of different groups.[32]

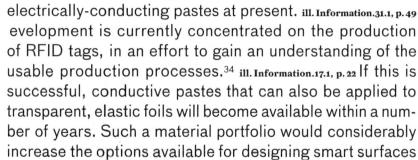

One notable version is a system developed at the University of Tokyo called *e-skin*. ill. Information.13.1, p.14 The material makes use of the conductivity of carbon nanotubes NANO Technical Background 5, p.83 and effectively combines the typical conductivity of metal with the characteristic elasticity of rubber. Nanoscale sensors or elastic circuits can be integrated in the matrix, allowing the material to be used either for energy transmission or as an artificial skin that is able to register warmth, or pressure, as required (as in robotics).[33]

Intensive research is also being conducted into ink-like, printable, electrically-conducting pastes at present. ill. Information.31.1, p.49 evelopment is currently concentrated on the production of RFID tags, in an effort to gain an understanding of the usable production processes.[34] ill. Information.17.1, p.22 If this is successful, conductive pastes that can also be applied to transparent, elastic foils will become available within a number of years. Such a material portfolio would considerably increase the options available for designing smart surfaces and skins. Complicated, inelastic media façade wiring systems could, for example, be replaced by conductive pastes. Different types of membrane constructions of variable transparency with integrated printed circuits are

conceivable, in combination, for instance, with energy- or light-generating printed surfaces.[35]

ill. Energy.13.1, p. 20; ENERGY Technical Background 1, p.89; LIGHT Technical Background 4.1, p. 112

31
Wenzel (2009), The inductive principle.
32
Optimistic estimations predict the imminent complete replacement of wire-bound power networks by inductive ones for single-family homes. Such scenarios may give rise to even more discussion about the possible effects of wireless networks on health. See Hochman (2009), Wireless Electricity is here (Seriously). Also: Hochman (2009), How Green is Wireless Electricity?
33
Sekitani et al. (2008), A Rubberlike Stretchable Active Matrix.
34
Arning et al. (2008), Printed Electronics.
35
Combinations with OLEDs and foil-based thin film solar cells are also conceivable.

2.4 Smart home

These dynamic technical developments are making it more and more necessary to consider comprehensive concepts for working and living environments using computer intelligence. Expressions like 'Smart Home'[36] refer to the classical single-family home in the sense of a system that can be used to verify initial experimental approaches, as well as an attractive market. It is nevertheless intended to apply the smaller-scale achievements to office buildings, hotels or hospitals in the medium-term.[37] The aim is to be able to develop a building control system that integrates daily, weekly and annual rhythms, and encompasses all household and entertainment devices, monitoring and security systems, heating, air-conditioning and ventilation systems, as well as all technical communication systems. ill. Information.15.1, p. 20 The

term can, however, also be used to include such diverse monitoring concepts as *Ambient Assisted Living*, which is dedicated to assisting people who are disabled, ill or in need of care.[38] ill. Information.30.1, p. 45 While the Smart Home approach tends to be overstretched at times, this application is certainly convincing.

The establishment of intelligent network standards is expected to have significant consequences for the implementation of the Smart Home idea. The definition of such network standards (protocols) for buildings is similar to the establishment of standards for data processing (e.g. *bluetooth*) or entertainment electronics, with which they are increasingly coordinated. The industry is mainly responsible for the development and agreement of such standards. Network standards such as the European Installation Bus (EIB),[39] the *Digital Addressable Lighting Interface* (DALI)[40] LIGHT Technical Background 2, p. 107 and the *Local Operating*

36
Other similar terms used include: intelligent home; e-home, or Internet home. 'Building automation' (BA) describes the whole field. For the history of the concepts, cf. Heckman (2008), Smart Houses and the Dream of the Perfect Day.

37
Examples of experimental research carried out on built objects include: the Fraunhofer Society's (Fraunhofer Gesellschaft) InHausII project, started in 2008; the MIT PlaceLab; and the temporary Media House Project in Barcelona, realised in 2003 by the same institution together with Spanish partners including the Metapolis architectural collective. For an overview of the respective research approaches please refer to: Grinewitschus (2007), Vernetzung optimieren. House_n Research Consortium (2005), Research Topics. MIT, 15 October 2005. Also Guallarte (2005), Media House Project.

38
Kunze et al. (2007), Ambient Assisted Living Anwendungen.

39
The European Installation Bus (EIB) is an EN 50090-compliant standard; the current version is the KNX Standard, also ISO/IEC 14543-3-compliant. KNX is the successor to three different bus systems, of which EIB (also its technical basis) is the most well-known. See www.knx.org.

40
See DALI Manual (2001).

Network (LON) regulate the installation and communication of technical components (e.g. electrical devices, lamps, window-blind motors). Sensors and actuators may also be included in the specifications. The networks are characterised by the flexible way in which end-users can address them. As opposed to a conventional circuit, the power supply and control are normally separated from each other in a consistently designed EIB network. A switch can therefore be programmed easily, without modifying the cable arrangement. The standardised wireless methods available to date, such as WLAN and bluetooth, are supplemented by another important standard called *ZigBee*. ZigBee is basically a protocol for (self-organising) sensor networks, i.e. it is targeted at wireless, short-range networks with low data rates, used for transmitting sensor information and control messages in building automation systems.[41]

3 Arduino, processing, wiring etc.

Almost diametrically opposed to the Smart Home concept is the very dynamic and prototypical field of information design,[42] promoted by the Internet and determining the whole course of development. 'Information design' encompasses bricolage, improvisation, temporary and experimental stages, as well as professional, integrative solution development.[43] This approach is documented in the previously mentioned work by Haque and Somlai ill. Information.25.3, p. 41 and is embodied in the abstract, but familiar-looking, intelligent *Blubber Bots*. ill. Information.01.1, p. 13; Information.01, p. 162 The increasing significance of open experimental platforms such as *Arduino, Processing* or *Wiring* in this respect can hardly be underestimated. These are mainly aimed at designers, artists and young programmers, allowing an introduction to technical experimentation and considerably facilitating the realisation of ideas and prototype

[41] Craig (2003), ZigBee.

[42] See Turner (2007), RoboHouse.

[43] Ramia Mazé is a design theoretician, who, following Lévi-Strauss, considers a re-emergence of bricolage, i.e. Do-It-Yourself (DIY) to be a significant force complementing the engineering science approach: "Via engineering and social science, 'bricolage' has influenced Human-Computer-Interface design (HCI), for example as 'improvisation' in learning, 'tinkering' in system developments, and 'tailoring' by end-users." Mazé (2007), Occupying Time, p. 66 An article in the magazine De:Bug. 'Electronic Aspects of Life' even considers the development to be a pop-culture phenomenon: "Rocket science for peanuts. [...] Now it is up to the creative mass of prosumers (producers-consumers) to create from the sea of raw materials available, that which art and culture always intended: to produce sense." Kubrick et al. (2008), Kluge Dinge. p. 13. Numerous blogs and forums (see appendix) as well as magazines such as Make or Craft reflect this development.

solutions. The different Arduino board models available[44] ill. Information.14.1, p. 18, ill. Information.33.1, p. 55 represent the programmable core component of a technical installation that is linked to other hardware components (sensors, actuators, LEDs). Both the hardware and the software are available under open-source licences. All designs and source texts are published and can be adapted to the user's own needs. A free-of-charge development environment for Linux, OS X and Windows is also available. Arduino can be considered to be a variant of the development environments *Processing*[45] and *Wiring*[46]. These are environments specialised for graphics, simulation and animation that can be used for programming interactions and visual elements and for designing Tangible User Interfaces. ill. Information.28.1, p. 43

44
Banzi (2008), Getting started with Arduino, O'Reilly 2008.
www.arduino.cc.
45
www.processing.org.
46
http://wiring.org.co.

PROJECTS

A

Nano.01
ACTIVE WINDOW
Hartmut Hillmer,
University of Kassel

ill. Nano.01.3, p. 52

The concept of the *Active Window*, which has been tested as a model, involves the modular, uniformly dense arrangement of sensor-controlled microscale mirrors (micromirror arrays) in the cavity space of conventional double glazing. Owing to their extremely small size (1,000 mirrors per square centimetre), the arrays resolve optically into a fine-meshed network that hardly affects the view. The *Active Window* combines the functions of dynamic daylight guidance and protection against direct sunlight and glare. The micromirrors are moved by means of electrostatic attractive forces generated through electrical voltage. Each individual mirror is mounted so as to move freely on a kind of leaf spring. They can be adjusted to any desired angle in relation to the sun by altering the voltage. The incident sunlight can be diverted to the ceiling to prevent glare and to prevent the room from heating up quickly. If there is nobody present in the room, the mirrors can also darken it completely. In winter, the solar radiation can be used to heat the room. A significantly improved distribution of brightness within interior rooms can be achieved through the *Active Window*. In principle, the rooms can be illuminated to outdoor daytime levels without direct sunlight. One key innovation is the simplification of the process steps (thin film technology with film thicknesses in the nanometre range) for the manufacturing the micromirrors, which are tested in projectors and scanners. Their widespread use now seems realistic, thanks to the development of suitable low-cost materials. System variants include combination with artificial lighting systems (LED arrays) and photovoltaic applications (as focusing elements). A 6 × 6 cm prototype module is being used to test the functional principle of nano-scale, sensor-controlled mirrors, which direct light with absolute precision and can, moreover, separate it into its spectral colours in a controlled way. The control of direction and colour value also make it possible to control the lighting atmosphere actively by carefully modulating it in order, for example, to simulate biorhythm-stimulating patterns of daylight during the autumn and winter, when natural lighting is more diffuse.

www.ina-kassel.de
Lit.: Hillmer et al. (2008), Sun Glasses for Buildings, pp. 135 – 139.

Surfaces.01
ADAPTIVE GENERATIVE PATTERN
Giorgos Artopoulos, Stanislav Roudavski
Cambridge University, UK

ill. Surfaces.01.2, p. 37

The case study *Adaptive Generative Pattern* describes a practice-oriented experimental trial of tessellation (tiling or decomposition) as a design tool. In this case, it has been used to build two computer-generated, organically-formed surface architectures for use as temporary exhibition objects. The principle of tessellation can be understood as the reduction of a topographic surface of complex form to a seamlessly coherent pattern of individual planes which, through the lower degree of complexity of the segments, makes it possible to address the overall relationship in a controlled way. In built form, the results resemble deformed honeycomb-shaped sandwich constructions. *Adaptive Generative Pattern* is based on the principle of decomposition illustrated by a Voronoi diagram, which determines the tessellation of space through a predetermined number of centres, producing a specific cell pattern. Following the computer-assisted determination of the pattern using a modelling program (FormZ, Maya) the precise surface topography is achieved through the two-dimensional processing (cutting pattern) of the three-dimensional connecting ribs that frame individual surfaces. Cardboard was chosen as the building material for *Adaptive Generative Pattern*. The connecting ribs were glued together in a technically simple yet labour-intensive process. The basic principle of adaptive pattern generation can be varied through the application of different decomposition principles. This makes possible the simulative design and construction of intelligent envelopes and surfaces according to natural growth principles or the transformation principles of physical and dynamic forces.

www.arct.cam.ac.uk/personal-page/stanislav_roudavski/index.html
Lit.: Artopoulos and Roudavski with François Penz (2006), Adaptive Generative Patterns, pp. 341 – 362.

Climate.01
A STYROFOAM LOVER WITH (E)MOTIONS OF CONCRETE
Susanne Zottl,
Vienna

ill. Climate.01.1, p. 53

As an alternative to the usual methods of thermal insulation involving unspecific layers of insulation material optimised for use on flat existing surfaces, the objects of the installation *A Styrofoam Lover with (E)Motions of Concrete* explore the insulation's design potential in the field of energy-efficient building. The prototypes created explore how existing or conceived uses can be combined with the requirements of insulation in the wall as a building component. Analogously to the function-concealing 'thick walls' of historical structures, which mediate between geometrically defined interiors and external built space through a sequence of development and small-scale spaces, these prototypes contain elements of the space allocation program, the new use. The material used is a mixture of recycled Styrofoam material, providing thermal insulation, and cement, which provides the elements with structural stability. There have been no previous attempts to use this special mixture, originally developed as horizontal supplementary insulation, in a space-defining sculptural form. A casting process was used in making the installation. The potential of this technology, in terms of spatial design, is enhanced by introducing a flexible skin as part of the formwork. The objects developed as part of the installation thus represent prototypes in respect of concept, material and construction. The aim of this ongoing work is to develop a consistent production technique.

www.zottlbuda.at
Lit.: Zottl (2009), A Styrofoam Lover, pp. 46–47.

B

Climate.02
BAD BY SMAQ
Sabine Müller and
Andreas Quednau,
Rotterdam

ill. Climate.02.3, p. 16

BAD (bath) is an architectural 'folly', a usable sculpture. It is based on an everyday summertime experience of energy generation: that the water in a garden hose left lying in the sun will heat up. The most conspicuous component of BAD is a meshwork formed of a hose system of 1000 metres in length which, as a water-filled, surface-maximised absorber, captures energy from the sun and heats up the water. It is designed according to the hose-in-hose principle. The transparent sheathing around the water-carrying hose acts as insulation and increases the efficiency of the absorber. The system's internal volume (content) corresponds to the amount of water required to fill the bathtub. In lightly overcast weather with an air temperature of 23°C, mains temperature water contained in an absorber plaited out of black hose heats up from 15°C to 47°C within around two hours. Yellow-red hose material was chosen to give the CNC-milled wooden framework construction a coherent appearance. The water used for bathing is subsequently used to water plants. BAD operates in a zone between dependency and self-sufficiency. The material qualities of the infrastructure necessary for its operation have been extrapolated to create ornamental architecture, simultaneously highlighting and exploring alternatives to the ways in which an urban landscape shaped by infrastructural realities and patterns of leisure is used.

www.smaq.net

Climate.03
BATWING
Emergent, Tom Wiscombe,
Josh Sprinkling, Alex Cornelius, Marcus Freisl,
Los Angeles

ill. Climate.03.3, p. 35

The *Batwing* design study should be seen in the wider context of studies devoted to the consistent design of the envelope, construction, and supply systems which constitute a building. Its aim is to develop an integrated design logic of a higher order, using bioconstructive geometries and atmospheric design. This logic should also express the independent system behaviour of the supporting structure and the technical, functional components of climate and light. The focus is less on optimising technology than on determining the key factors (in terms of the effect of an object and of translucency, formal viscosity, sheen and silhouette) through which the spatial experience of architecture can be united with the infrastructural necessities, beyond the mere display of ducts and cables, to create a whole that can be experienced through the senses. The form results from a process of surface transformation (pleating) which, in determining the relationships between structural hardness and directed airflow, creates ornamental patterns. During the creation of the building envelope, a duct system is formed, which supplies intake air and ensures the structural continuity of the façade elements. Deep pleats form air diffusers that contain a microcapillary solar thermal system for cooling and heating the airflow, thus replacing centrally-controlled air-conditioning systems. The design language of *Batwing* is consciously influenced by the system-integrative surface viscosity of automobiles and aircraft and the design-sensitive construction methods of geometrically extreme forms being experimented with here.

www.emergentarchitecture.com
Lit.: Wiscombe (2009), Bioconstructivism, p. 43.

Nano.02
BIG SPLASH
Lydéric Bocquet,
Université de Lyon

ill. Nano.02.1, p. 51

The research group Liquids@Interface, headed by physicist Lydéric Bocquet, is involved in the experimental study of the hydrodynamic behaviour of nanostructured surfaces. The *Big Splash* study illustrates the functional principle of nanotechnical thin-layer processes and effects. Two glass balls with different coatings, but which are otherwise identical, create clearly distinctive splash patterns when immersed quickly in water. Their reactive behaviour, ranging from hydrophilic to hydrophobic, can be adjusted by treating the surface. The hydrophilic ball, wet with hydrogen peroxide, sulphuric acid and alcohol, produces virtually no splash as it enters the water, whereas the hydrophobic (water-repellent) ball, coated with a thin layer of silane, creates a big splash.

www-lpmcn.univ-lyon1.fr/~lbocquet
Lit.: Bocquet et al. (2007), Making a splash, pp. 180–183.

Information.01
BLUBBER BOTS
Jed Berk,
Los Angeles

ill. Information.01.1, p. 13

The airy *Blubber Bots* are designed very simply yet behave intelligently. Controlled by light- and pressure-sensitive sensors, piezoacoustic actuators (loudspeakers), LEDs and electric-motor-driven propellers (sensor-actuator system) they resemble a friendly, socially-conscious species of robot in the way they interact with objects, surroundings and people. The zeppelin-like, helium-filled Bots react to light impulses and detected mobile phone signals rather like insects. They can receive messages communicated via the interface of a mobile phone and respond to them by means of flashing signals, by altering their position in the room, or (via loudspeakers integrated in the Mylar envelope) with a whale-like song. They register obstacles in the vicinity via contact sensors. The *Blubber Bots* can be understood as an experimental form of collective intelligence, by means of which abstract principles relating to the network-based communication of information can be tested.

www.alavs.com

C

Light.01
COCOON CLUB
3deluxe,
Wiesbaden

ill. Light.01.1, p. 26

The *Cocoon Club* is a playground for architectural experimentation, in which the multi-sensory perception of the interior is constantly changed under the influence of moving light. A perforated wall area about 100 m in length encloses the main room and acts as the projection surface for a 360° light installation. The multi-layered wall structure calls to mind the organic structure of a permeable cell membrane. It is pierced by 13 capsular microspaces (cocoons), visually linking the active inner area with the quieter outer area. Altogether, 23 beamers project pre-programmed textures and animations onto the coloured fine concrete elements that make up the projection surface, using specially developed interfaces (touch screen, glass sculpture, bongos). The intensive and dynamic effect of the light is enhanced by black varnished acoustic mats on the ceiling and a dark wooden floor. Specific areas can be excluded or highlighted with various masks in a 3D computer model. Light can also be directed to the front or rear layer of the wall surface in this way. A computer network allows real time synchronisation of the projections, the show lighting and the sound. The perfect blending of this digital layer makes the membrane wall look alive: the surface seems to surrender its material nature and dissolve into light.

www.3deluxe.de
Lit.: 3deluxe (2009), Transdisciplinary Approaches to Design.

of the connecting passageways of the museum with sunlight.

At night, the façade is transformed into a dynamic sheet of light that can be seen from afar, enhanced by its reflection in the river. The pixels can be addressed individually and the low resolution factor is compensated by using white light, resulting in a very elegant appearance. As in the retina of the eye, image definition varies in different areas of the façade. This is achieved by the irregular density of picture elements integrated in one of three possible types of façade panel. The idea of combining different resolutions in a façade system can partly be attributed to the realisation by the designers of Realities United that it's not really the eye that 'sees', but the brain.

www.nietosobejano.com
www.realities-united.de

Light.02
COMMUNICATIVE LIGHTING FAÇADE (EASTERN FAÇADE)
Nieto Sobejano Arquitectos
in cooperation with Realities United,
Madrid and Berlin

ill. Light.02.1, p. 30

This competition-winning design by Nieto Sobejano will decorate the eastern, river façade of the *Cordoba Centre of Contemporary Art* with a light and media façade. Standing at the edge of the Rio Guadalquivir, the building is practically predestined for just this. The new façade will be visible for several hundred metres. Realities United designers were commissioned to develop the light and media façade in cooperation with the architects.

The perforated surface of the façade reflects the hexagonal and interlaced structures of the museum. It consists of polygonal relief panels, pre-cast from fibre-reinforced concrete; these indirectly illuminated bowl-shaped structures also form the individual pixels of the media surface. Produced in various sizes, they do not appear to follow any kind of logical arrangement; only the density of hollows within the area of each façade panel is balanced. It has not yet been decided whether the lighting control (in a manner analogous to reflector technology) should be optimised by processing the inward-sloping bowl surfaces, either by milling the fibre concrete surface, or by applying a ceramic microstructured surface.

The disappointing daytime banality of many architectural media structures is not encountered here: the structured façade of the museum offers an impressive interplay of shadow and light under natural lighting conditions. The relief-structured wall perforations also allow indirect illumination

Nano.03
CONSTRUCTION IN VIVO
Neri Oxman and A. John Hart,
MIT Cambridge, MA,
University of Michigan

ill. Nano.03.3, p. 29

Construction in Vivo is a visionary prototypical concept of a material architecture created through the hierarchical combination of carbon nanotubes (CNTs), polymers and conventional building materials such as steel, wood and glass, the reactions of which to climatic environmental influences are not mechanically actuated, that is to say: it behaves like a multifunctional skin. Different technical methods (form-oriented CNT growth, 3D printing and lay-up technologies) are combined to generate an inherently nanostructured macro-surface. This consists of a ribbed structure of densely packed CNTs impregnated with structured epoxy resin, representing the load-bearing zones, while the permeable zones are of a tissue-like transparent composite, formed of melted glass particles and nanotechnically generated electrodes, electrochromic oxides and electroactive polymer molecules organised as a spatial multilayer.

Starting out from the supporting skeleton, this structure is fabricated in a single piece. The functional behaviours are created *in vivo* through the material architecture, i.e. they are adjusted through directed growth of the nanotubes and polymers, organised on the micro and nano level, which form the material. Such a material could be formed in a differentiated way, depending on the context, i.e. it could contain numerous structures within itself simultaneously, or change its degree of transparency in order, for example, to regulate the light in individual rooms, or else open individual pores in order to ventilate a room, and, ideally and potentially, supply itself with energy.

www.constructioninvivo.com
www.materialecology.com
www.nanobliss.com
Lit.: ACADIA 08 (2008), Silicon + Skin.

Energy.01
CROWD FARM
James Graham and
Thaddeus Jusczyk,
MIT Cambridge, MA

ill. Energy.01.1, p. 39

The project aims to use the kinetic energy generated by the movement of crowds of people in urban environments. A subfloor made of plates that are able to move against each other, if installed in the lobby of a railway station, for instance, can produce electricity using the friction developed between the elements as a result of human motion. While the pulse generated by a single step is only enough to power two 60 W bulbs for one second, the steps of a whole crowd add up to a significant electric current. The authors use Boston's South Station terminal to illustrate how their as yet hypothetical *Crowd Farm* system of generating energy would work. 30,000 steps would correspond to the energy required to power a train for one second.

http://sap.mit.edu/resources/portfolio/crowd_farm
Lit.: Priya, Inman (2008), Energy Harvesting Technologies.

D

Surfaces.02
DO HIT
Marijn van der Poll,
Eindhoven

ill. Surfaces.02.1, p. 51

The *Do hit* chair elevates the tense contrast between craftsmanship and industrially manufactured semifinished product to the level of a concept. The starting form for the *Do hit* is a simple metal cube made of sheet steel which is formed into a chair by means of hammer blows according to the creator's individual motivation. The process is based on the idea of creative destruction, according to which an object is given its ideal form (surface) through deliberate destruction.

www.marijnvanderpoll.com

Energy.02
DRIP FEED
Thomas Raynaud and
Cyrille Berger,
Paris

ill. Energy.02.1, p. 47

There is an island of about 31 hectares called Sacca San Mattia in the Venetian Lagoon that has not really been used for anything special in the past, apart from dumping waste and debris from building work carried out in the historical centre. The idea is to convert the area into an energy-generating urban park that can also be visited by tourists. A network of kilometres of parallel pipes spans the island like a green tent. The colour is due to the culture of green algae *(Ulva rigida)* inside the pipes. Underneath this penetrable layer, the lagoon biotope is preserved and remains open to prevailing weather conditions. Various facilities are provided for visitors in the park. The multifunctional bioreactor produces biomass for energy generation, seaweed for human consumption, and oxygen for enrichment of the water in the lagoon, while at the same time actively binding CO_2 created by the refineries located on the edge of the lagoon. The design unites the interests of environmental protection and tourism. *Drip Feed* acts as a biofilter counteracting the destruction of the lagoon. At the same time, it represents an important contribution to the development of efficient and sustainable tourism concepts in Venice.

www.buildingbuilding.org
Lit.: Fitzwilly (2009), Make a Microbial Fuel Cell (MFC). Granel, Turner (2006),
Ecology of Harmful Algae. Richmond (2004),
Handbook of Microalgal Culture.

Information.02
ECHOLOGUE
Orkan Telhan,
MIT Cambridge, MA

ill. Information.02.1, p. 31

The prototype of the *Echologue* displays consists of twelve triangular, flexibly-connected segments, equipped on both sides with white LEDs (pixels), which when two segments are combined to form a square produce a resolution of 32 × 32 = 1024 pixels. This design allows the strip-like ambient display to be suspended freely in space in ever-new ways; it can be moved by its users and reshaped according to the principles of segment logic. The display is equipped with acoustic sensors. Ambient noises are reproduced as an optical echo, i.e. as animated, non-figurative, calligraphic, zoomorphic patterns in shades of grey, coordinated over all of the segments. The *Echologue* deliberately avoids the aggressive use of technology. Using the means of technical, visual and geometric spatial abstraction and reduction, it induces spontaneous, socially communicative actions in a public space.

www.orkantelhan.info
Lit.: Telhan (2007), Social Sensing and its Display.

Energy.03
ENERGY FARM – HYDROGEN PLATFORM
Marcel Lehmann,
BTU Cottbus

ill. Energy.03.1, p. 55

The *Hydrogen Platform* project involves a prototype hydrogen production facility to supply a city of about 100,000 inhabitants. The pilot plant, located in the middle of a former open-pit mining area, is fed by a range of sources of regenerative energy (biomass, wind, sun), from which hydrogen is generated in various ways. The platform also represents an intervention in the landscape. The individual phases of the energy transformation process can be understood in terms of the arrangement of three minimised structures. Biomass is converted to a synthesis gas in a fluidised bed reactor located in a wall structure. Pipes conduct the gas upwards

to machines and equipment at the base of a 170 m long flat horizontal structure on the upper edge of the open pit mine. The upper part of the horizontal structure is a transparent absorber for harvesting solar energy. Just behind the glass façade, living biomass consisting of a culture of green algae is used for the continuous production of highly pure hydrogen. The gas obtained from various sources is finally distributed via different routes. The majority is transferred to the regional gas supply network, where it is converted to electricity and thermal energy by means of fuel cells in existing converter stations, and fed into the existing infrastructure. The remaining hydrogen is liquefied in the plant and prepared for transport by road. Liquid hydrogen is a major product available at hydrogen filling stations in addition to hydrogen gas.

www.ls-aoe.tu-cottbus.de
www.smartsurfaces.de
Lit.: Fitzwilly (2009), Make a Microbial Fuel Cell (MFC). Granel, Turner (2006), Ecology of Harmful Algae. Richmond (2004), Handbook of Microalgal Culture.

Surfaces.03
FIBER ARCHITECTURE
Tokujin Yoshioka,
Tokyo

ill. Surfaces.03.1, p. 45

Weaving involves the creation of space through nothing other than surface. *Fiber Architecture* is the vision of a space-forming structure which, rather than owing its strength (which conveys a feeling of security) to conventionally hard, solid materials, seeks to achieve a surprising strength from the intelligently organised combination of fine and lightweight elements (fibres), which leads to an idiosyncratic expression of the whole. *Fiber Architecture* follows the ideal of the Japanese Aikido as an art of defence which uses the force of the attack and transforms it into the defender's strength. This design approach derives its strength from the ambiguity of the term 'fibre', which refers to different things in different sub-disciplines. In nature and technology, fibres are usually found combined in large numbers. They form a particular structure which, as a rule, results in stronger and frequently more rigid constructions than the same form made of a homogenous material. In information technology, glass fibres are used as cable material. *Fiber Architecture* represents the search for new manifestations of surface intelligence in the symbiotic combination of supporting structure and network.

http://tokujin.com

Surfaces.04
FIDU
Oskar Zieta,
ETH Zurich

ill. Surfaces.04.1, p.15

Since its introduction, sheet metal has always been worked by subjecting it to pressure, stamping it with massive force in dies or impressing it with stamps. As a genuine industrial surface material, it is always designed for high performance and, despite its light weight, provides maximum stability, precision and formal freedom. The acronym *FIDU* stands for "Freie Innen Druck Umformung (Free Internal Pressure Deformation)" and refers to an innovative process involving the deformation of thin, two-layered steel sheeting in order to create extremely stable three-dimensional elements by means of internally-generated hydraulic or air pressure. The method competes with standard processes, since it allows the use of significantly lower pressures, as well as comparatively easily accessible technologies and equipment. The final form is controlled by means of the geometry (outline shape) of the pre-cut blank and the internal pressure used. Laser-cutting, as an ideal universal cutting and joining process, is the first production step. Once cut to shape, the steel sheets are joined, pressure-tight, using welding robots controlled by computer or by manual scanning. The welded shapes are inflated by introducing water into the intermediate space. Regulation of the hydraulic pressure (6 to 50 bar), depending on the geometry and thickness of the material, determines the degree of deformation. The resulting form remains stable after the water is drained off. With the same expenditure of material, the forms created in this way are many times more stable than comparable elements made from folded sheet metal. The *FIDU* method also allows non-linear and complex deformations and produces a formal language not previously associated with sheet metals. Further development focuses on the process step of deformation as a reproducible process for the generation of lightweight and stable architectural constructions, which can be controlled in all its parameters.

www.blech.arch.ethz.ch
Lit.: FIDU eine neue Verarbeitungsmethode im Blech (2009).

Light.03
FLARE
WHITEvoid,
Berlin

ill. Light.03.2, p. 24

While most media façades communicate using artificial light, the dynamic media façade developed in the *Flare* project does this with a mechanical surface. Ambient light is reflected by a modular system that consists of a great number of individually movable metal surfaces; the degree of reflection depends on the inclination of each surface. The façade composed of these small segments is therefore able to display a broad range of shades, from very light to very dark.

A basic module covers one square meter and consists of four polygonal structures (flakes). Pneumatic pistons allow the individual control of the modules, which are positioned to achieve the required inclination. The polygonal structures making up the façade give it a three-dimensional appearance, even when viewed from the side. An otherwise static façade is turned into a 'living' skin that is able to react interactively to activities inside and outside the building, thanks to an ingenious computerised control system.

www.whitevoid.com

Nano.04
FUNCTIONAL COATINGS
EFDS e.V.,
Dresden

ill. Nano.04.1, p. 13

Using the fundamental nanotechnology of the thin-layer process, the material and functional properties of materials can be deliberately and significantly influenced by modifying their surface characteristics. The majority of the nano-applications currently used in design and building involve enhancing the functionality of surfaces. Thin layers can also be used for decorative purposes, in the form of coloured interference coatings. These are transparent oxide layers of high brilliance, whose colour value depends on the thickness of the layer and varies according to the viewing angle. However, the main focus of attention is on the application of transparent protective coatings: protection against corrosion, abrasion and scratching, against light and thermal radiation, against heat loss, against soiling and bacterial contamination. The known cleaning effects (easy-to-clean, anti-misting, lotus effect) are, for the most part, based on the principle of photocatalysis, in which the coating is stimulated by UVA radiation to undergo oxidation or chemical reduction processes (photo-induced hydrophilia caused by sunlight, or fluorescent light) which in turn cause organic and inorganic substances on the surface to decompose. Thin interference coatings can increase the light reflection value of diffusely reflective surfaces (light guidance systems, bulb reflectors) by over 20 per cent. In a similar way, anti-reflective coatings on the glass covers of solar modules reduce losses due to the reflection of solar radiation, increasing their efficiency by up to five per cent.www.efds.de, www.ls-aoe.tu-cottbus.de,

www.smartsurfaces.de

Lit.: Europäische Forschungsgemeinschaft Dünne Schichten EFDS e. V. et al. (2004), Material Change. Klooster (2005), Functional Surfaces, pp. 103–106.

weight (saving material) and high resistance to corrosion, which could be erected in a comparatively short time. Even now, materials such as *G.crete.ultra* are already opening up design options that are unusual for concrete. The variants of UHPC are characterised by very high resilience, strength, density and resistance to abrasion. The material is not subject to any limitations in terms of form and shape. It allows extraordinarily small building component cross sections of 3 mm, as well as the creation of differently formed, structured (rough, matt, dense, shiny) or coloured surfaces. In addition to load-bearing structural components, it can be used for producing innovative surface components such as façade elements (curtain walls), panels, slabs or tiles.

Lit.: Zimmermann, Grohmann (2008), Membrane concrete grid shells (UHPC). Zimmermann et al. (2007), In:Ex:terior Structures.

G

Surfaces.05
G.CRETE.ULTRA (UHPC)
Gtecz,
Kassel

ill. Surfaces.05.2, p. 57

The concrete material *G.crete.ultra* is a building material belonging to the class of ultra high-strength concretes (Ultra High Performance Concrete—UHPC) currently under development. These are distinguished by a compressive strength that is greater, by a factor of ten, than that of conventional concrete and which corresponds roughly to that of steel. The technological basis involves increasing the structural density of the material, consisting of cement, aggregates, water and additives, which can be understood as a strength-increasing minimisation of the spaces between the substance particles at the micro to nano scale (molecular level). With optimal manufacture and aftertreatment, UHPC displays virtually no pores or microcracks. It is practically watertight. Research into ultra high-strength concretes is aimed at producing a material with the elasticity, compressive and tensile strength ("better than steel") and surface consistency (density and hardness) of ceramic materials while retaining the positive basic properties of concrete (working, fire behaviour). Structures built of UHPC would be distinguished by extraordinarily delicate, lightweight supporting structures of low dead

Nano.05
GECKO GLUE
Liming Dai, Zhong Lin Wang,
University of Dayton, GeorgiaTech

ill. Nano.05.1, p. 26

With their millions of superfine hairs, the adhesive pads on the gecko's feet develop barely measurable forces of attraction (van der Waals forces) to the substrate and give it the fascinating ability to climb vertical walls. They are the model for *Gecko Glue*, a tissue-like technical surface consisting of a directionally grown structure of vertically oriented nanotubes with horizontally spiralling ends which, due to their arrangement and the electrostatic properties of the tubes, develop an extraordinary adhesive strength. The prototype of a 3 × 3 cm large strip can support up to 100 kilograms and sticks dry to various surfaces (sandpaper, glass, plastic). It can be used reversibly. A wide range of applications are conceivable, from substituting magnets and equipping wall-climbing service robots to making high-strength flexible connections for building components and the façade elements of demountable structures.

http://academic.udayton.edu/LimingDai
www.nanoscience.gatech.edu/zlwang
Lit.: Dai, Wang et al. (2008), Carbon Nanotube Arrays with Strong Shear Binding-On, p. 238.

Light.04
GREENPIX—ZERO ENERGY
MEDIA WALL
Simone Giostra & Partners with Arup, New York

ill. Light.04.3, p. 21

The *GreenPix—Zero Energy Media Wall* is a media façade with a photovoltaic system: a combination that makes it possible to operate 2,200 m² of display area without any additional energy being required. 2,292 coloured LEDs are arranged in 89 × 89 cm arrays behind the translucent glass sheet of the curtain wall façade. The polycrystalline photovoltaic cells laminated within the point-fixed, composite glass of the curtain wall fulfil two functions: energy generation and sun protection. The density with which the cells are arranged on the building's skin varies, allowing the rooms located behind the media wall to be illuminated with natural light as required by their use. The irregular, decorative distribution of the photovoltaic cells gives the façade a structured appearance during the day. The solar energy harvested during the day is used for various purposes within the building. Surplus energy is stored to be emitted as light via the media envelope at night. User-specific software allows the intelligent skin of the building to interact with the public. The dynamic images displayed are exclusively artistic and the programme is under professional supervision. The appearance of the façade is characterised by an extraordinarily high light intensity and a low display resolution.

www.greenpix.org
Lit.: Sinclair Eakin (2007), A Gleam in the Eye, pp. 47 – 48.

Energy.04
GROW
SMIT Sustainably Minded Interactive Technology, New York

ill. Energy.04.2, p. 18

Grow is a hybrid energy-generating system, converting both solar and wind energy to electricity. Each one of the 'solar leaves' of the system is a micro-power station in itself. The leaves are attached to building façades, rather like climbing ivy.

Grow.1 makes use of flexible thin film solar cells as well as piezoelectric technology. The design being developed is based on thin film solar cells with piezoelectric generators and screen-printed conductive ink encapsulated in ETFE (ethylene tetrafluoroethylene) fluoropolymer lamination. These are arranged in a type of modular brick system. Each brick holds five collector leaves with a flexible piezoelectric generator at their stem. Each element can be replaced easily at the end of its life cycle; old elements can be split up into their basic material components and to a large extent recycled.

Grow.2 on the other hand does not rely on piezoelectric power generation. The system is almost ready for the market. It uses only flexible thin film solar cells manufactured by, likewise encapsulated in ETFE and attached to a corrosion-protected steel mesh system. The 100 % recyclable polyethylene leaves can be given different colours.

http://s-m-i-t.com

H

Climate.04
HIGH PERFORMANCE
MASONRY WALL SYSTEM
Jason Vollen, Rensselear CASE, New York

ill. Climate.04.1, p. 51

Against the background of increasing encroachment upon the fragile ecosystem of the south-western USA, the *High Performance Masonry Wall System* case study addresses the development of a prototypical system of modules made of ceramic materials with a special cross section. The structure of the module's surface is designed so as to combine the regulated storage behaviour of local desert cacti (barrel cactus) and the thermal ventilation behaviour of termite mounds in response to climate. In principle, the barrel cactus functions like a living cistern. The circulating stored water supplies the plant during dry periods and distributes the heat load. In contrast to the generally accepted logic that requires buildings to minimise the ratio of envelope to volume, the skin of the cactus is highly differentiated in form. During a drought the cactus shrinks, creating cooling ridges that shade the surface. Changes in colour over the growth period allow the reflective behaviour of the skin to be adapted to the seasons. Termite mounds, for their part, are taller or flatter depending on the location. Their geometry is context-related and is designed to allow heat storage or cooling through the circulation of air. Like the models studied, the *High Performance Masonry Wall System* is optimised in terms of form, proportion of openings, surface geometry and glazing, with a view to controlling solar heat gain and ventilation behaviour (evaporation). Starting out from the efficient storage properties of ceramics as a building material (heat, moisture), the different zones, which are highly differentiated in form, are activated or deactivated as the shading of the façade (self-shading) changes over the course of the seasons. Adjusted in this way, the *High Performance Masonry Wall* regulates the building's interior climate through the overall behaviour of the facade, the airflows that occur and incident solar radiation, without the need for additional technical systems.

www.case.rpi.edu
Lit.: Vollen, Jason et al. (2008), High Performance Masonry Wall Systems.

Information.03
THE HUG SHIRT
Cutecircuit Ltd.,
London

ill. Information.03.1, p. 42

The Hug Shirt demonstrates principles of Smart Clothing and the design of Tangible User Interfaces (TUI, Interaction Design). A system of sensors integrated in the shirt registers the wearer's skin temperature and pulse, and measures the duration and intensity of pressure impulses on the surface of the skin, such as those induced by the wearer 'hugging him/herself'. The data thus registered can be instantaneously captured and transmitted to a specified recipient via the Bluetooth network of a mobile phone. The Hug Shirt of the person receiving this set of data uses actuators to reproduce the hug sent by phone. The sensor-actuator system is designed as an application and can be removed. This means that the Hug Shirt is washable. The systematic structure of the components as sensor and actuator, Bluetooth network and mobile phone, including the Java programming implemented on it, which together produce an intuitive interface design for use in a playful way, is exemplary.

www.cutecircuit.com

Climate.05
HYDRO WALL
Virginia San Fratello,
Oakland

ill. Climate.05.2, p. 48

The *Hydro Wall* is a sophisticated system of façade components formed of concrete and plastics (thermoplastics), which is designed to collect, filter and store rain water. Conceived, in terms of its dimensions, more for a temperate-to-hot climate, the Hydro Wall uses water stored in rubber bladders within the wall as an active thermal mass (solar thermal principle). The water is heated by the sun's rays and can be used, directly or on a phase-controlled basis (e.g. in a day-night rhythm), for room climate control (heating and cooling) or to cover general hot water requirements. The concept combines the principles of energy-efficient design with the potential offered by experimental form-finding processes.

www.rael-sanfratello.com

L

Climate.06
LIVING GLASS
The Living, Soo-in Yang and
David Benjamin,
New York

ill. Climate.06.1, p. 28

The functional principle of the *Living Glass* kinetic climate control system is based on a sensor-actuator system that measures the carbon dioxide content of the room air and, when limit values are reached, opens and closes gill-like slits in the transparent silicone membrane. The inflow of fresh air is regulated by wires made of a shape-memory alloy, which are induced to contract by the application of a voltage. In comparison with other kinetic walls, *Living Glass* is characterised by its thin, very lightweight integrated construction, which does not require any motors or mechanically moved parts. The components of the movement system are laid in the still-liquid silicone in the mould during the manufacture of the membrane, so that the system is embedded in the surface. The wire used as an artificial muscle, called Flexinol or Musclewire, is a special variant of the shape-memory alloy Nitinol and is optimised for such actuator applications. It can be deformed up to a million times. When a voltage is applied, heat is generated in the wire, causing it to contract. An expanding counterforce develops as soon as it begins to cool. The realistic full-size prototype proves the practicability of *Living Glass*. With only minor modifications, it can be used for the climate control of objects and rooms.

www.thelivingnewyork.com
Lit.: Mills (1992), Stiquito. Conrad (2005), Stiquito Controlled!

M

Climate.07
MASSIVE SKIN
Sven Hansen and Philipp Thole,
BTU Cottbus

ill. Climate.07.1, p. 50

The project study *Massive Skin* illustrates the idea of a thin film that has the thermal properties of a massive wall. Via a translucent layer of microscopically encapsulated PCMs (heat storage layer), minute trumpet-shaped sails regulate the incident solar radiation and the climatic behaviour of the system as a whole. These trumpets, which have a funnel-shaped cross section and are vapour-coated with a reflective thin layer, open in the air flow. When extended, they combine the functions of sun protection and insulation with that of a concentrator which guides incident solar radiation on to the level of the PCMs. The resulting thermal energy can then, depending on the context, be radiated inwards passively or used actively via an integrated capillary system. The polymer material of the selectively permeable PCM carrier film contains electroluminescent pigments, which are excited by UV radiation. As darkness starts to fall, the film begins to glow, so reducing the energy consumption for artificial lighting. In the logic of its layer structure, materiality and geometry of the components, *Massive Skin* exemplifies a thermally activated, adaptive climate membrane.

www.ls-aoe.tu-cottbus.de
www.smartsurfaces.de

Information.04
MEDIABALLS
Christan Rothe, Kay Michalczack,
BTU Cottbus

ill. Information.04.2, p. 15

Mediaballs is the name of a low-cost, prototype media façade system—created using the cheapest, mass-produced, electrotechnical products—for the dynamic display of scrolling text on the principle of passive light reflection. The system consists of commercially-available table tennis balls, chrome-plated with spray paint, which are moved back and forth in a grid board of black Perspex with the aid of doorbell clappers. The chrome plating of the balls serves to improve the reflection of ambient light and thus the legibility of the displayed text. Each ball (pixel) can be individually actuated, microtechnically, through the movement mechanism of the clapper. When a *Mediaball* receives a control impulse, it moves suddenly from its resting position inside the Perspex cylinder to project halfway out of the grid board, and back again. *Mediaballs* can be used to animate text, images and simple movement sequences in a pixel pattern. The prototype of the scrolling text display can currently be manufactured at a quarter of the cost of an LED scrolling display. The biggest cost factor is the microtechnical control.

www.ls-aoe.tu-cottbus.de
www.smartsurfaces.de

Information.05
THE MEDIA HOUSE
Iaac with MIT Media Lab,
Barcelona, Cambridge, MA

ill. Information.05.1, p. 58

Represented diagrammatically, the operating logic of a network-based computer architecture (server architecture) resembles a space frame formed of rods. Building on this congruence of supporting structure and network, the test set-up of the *Media House*, which mirrors the requirements of a single-family house, is, in its built form, largely determined through the virtual architecture of the computer. The 'genetic code' of the house is formed of thumbnail-sized microtechnical components (microservers) in the nodes of the supporting structure, which is formed of standardised rods equipped with multiphase busbars. The microservers form the network nodes of the house and, on the basis of a simplified modification of the standard internet protocol, allow the free arrangement, reconfiguration and independent microtechnical control of all media (service engineering) components (IT, lighting and electrical, climate, control engineering, water). The changeable room structure is thus in every respect pervaded by the flexible, decentralised network intelligence of the internet. The *Media House* graphically illustrates the potential of modern network standards (protocols) and bus systems for buildings such as those of the *Digital Addressable Lighting Interface* DALI (lighting) or the European Installation Bus EIB (now KNX, electrical). These networks are characterised by the flexible addressability of the end consumers. This means, for example, that a switch can be reprogrammed using simple means and, in the case of the *Media House*, reassigned freely on the multiphase busbars without any need to alter the cable connections. The *Media House* overrides the clear division which currently prevails between the work of architects, which determines the physical form of the room, and that of the specialist engineers responsible for the infrastructure (network architects). Room design, lighting design and interaction design become a single act. Creative decisions in the digital world become simultaneously effective in the real world, and vice versa.

www.iaac.net
Lit.: Guallarte (2005), Media House Project.

Surfaces.06
MENSA—ELASTIC SPACE (POLYURETHANE)
J. Mayer H.,
Berlin

ill. Surfaces.06.1, p. 34

Beyond its technical potential in terms of the physical and chemical protection of materials, the intelligent principle of coating permits a play with meanings. Through the correct choice of coating, a surface can acquire depth in both the material and the semantic sense. In the same way, everything which stands in the way of the spatial effect can be toned down. Coatings can be used to widen or narrow, accentuate and generally challenge our perception of spaces. Of particular interest are the activating effects of spatially continuous surfaces in terms of communicative and functional processes. As a space of defined permeability, the design of the *Mensa* student canteen built in a central location on the campus of Karlsruhe University negotiates the identities of three faculties, the adjacent urban fabric and a nearby area of natural woodland.

The essentially elastic form is determined by model processes of morphological transformation of a discretely continuous structure, which in its definitive form forms a pattern which remains ambiguous. The continuity of surfaces essential for the building to function is achieved through using a shaped wooden construction whose excess of visual information is filtered by means of a seamless, sprayed-on polyurethane coating, which almost completely covers the building. Polyurethane was originally developed more than twenty years ago for the reliable sealing of building components exposed to extreme conditions (parking decks, flat roofs) and its material properties are almost ideal for this application. It is particularly resistant to pressure and abrasion, impact and shock; it is open to diffusion, resistant to ageing, temperature and chemicals, moreover it is root-proof and can be dyed almost any colour. A coating, applied by spraying, bonds fully with the substrate and forms a durable seal. An exemplary reciprocal relationship exists between the increase in the intensity of the forms resulting from the use of polyurethane and the development of a distinctive constructive approach that is characterised by the simplification of structural transitions and joints.

www.jmayerh.de.
Lit.: Finckh (2004), Surfaces semantisch/functional.

N

Energy.05
NANO VENT-SKIN
Agustin Otegui Saiz,
Mexico-City

ill. Energy.05.2, p. 42

Nano Vent-Skin (NVS) is a design study that constitutes a far-reaching interpretation of the scientifically predicted potential of 'hard' and 'soft' nanoengineering. *NVS* is made out of micro-turbines, each 25 mm long and 10.8 mm wide, with turbine surfaces that are bioactive on the interior and otherwise are light-active. They are thus able to generate electricity from wind and sunlight, while at the same time acting as a biofilter for air-borne pollutants. The outer skin of the structure absorbs sunlight using organic solar cell technology and transports the resulting energy to storage units at the panel juncture points through nanofibres within nanowires, lending the *NVS* structural support. Independently of this, the turbines generate electric current by their wind-induced rotation. The voltage created in this manner is potentiated by means of electrochemically active microorganisms on the bioactive upper side of the nanowires and transformed before it too is conducted to the storage units. The inner skin of each turbine acts as a CO2 filter, cleaning air as it passes through the *NVS*. Each panel has contact with four storage and supply units. These units act as control centres and ensure correct operation. They send building material (microorganisms) to repair faulty turbines, as well as receiving and storing the generated energy. *Nano Vent-Skin* is a highly efficient 'zero emission material'—a product of nanobiotechnology and nanoengineering. On account of its inconspicuousness, large areas of *NVS* can be mounted in many different places. The predicted action is demonstrated particularly well by structures naturally exposed to large wind energies, such as the façades of high-rise buildings and the surfaces of railway or subway train tunnel systems.

www.agustin-otegui.com

Information.06
NEW SENSUAL INTERFACES
Chris Woebken,
New York

ill. Information.06.1, p.43

The conceptual approach of *New Sensual Interfaces* derives its principle of *organic electronics* from current discourses. Linseeds are used to simulate minute units with biosensory intelligence from which similarly intuitive interfaces, arising from the user's personal actions and thinking, can be created, opening up completely new ways of interacting with digital data. The Sensual Interface can be understood as an extrapolation of the technological 'sketches' of Smart Dust and Utility Fog. Sensual design and poetic forms of interaction are developed by means of speculative prototypes. Taking seeds which, in nature, contain all the materials and information required for complex biological growth processes, and using them to simulate Smart Dust makes it possible, for example, to demonstrate new interactive forms of data mining (displacing, separating, dividing, discarding). In their methodology, the New *Sensual Interfaces* generate new ways of behaving and help to redefine our stereotypical relationship with electronics and with electronic building components and products.

www.woebken.net
Lit.: Woebken (2009), Sensual Interfaces.
Storrs Hall (1996), Utility Fog, pp. 161 – 184.

Climate.08
NON-LOAD-BEARING EXTERNAL WALL SYSTEMS WITH INTEGRATED VACUUM INSULATION SYSTEMS
Jan Cremers,
Munich

ill. Climate.08.2, p. 59

Whereas virtually all previous applications of vacuum insulation panels (VIPs) treat them merely as substitutes for conventional insulation materials in familiar forms of construction, Jan Cremers' case study demonstrates possibilities for developing consistent new construction principles based on the characteristic features of the VIP. The basic system addresses the weaknesses of VIPs. They can only be deformed to a limited extent, only withstand pressure if it is spread over a large area, and cannot simply be drilled through. Cremers therefore decided to suspend the system (suspended façade) and to complete the construction using a minimum of elements, all lightweight. A key decision was to offset two layers of VIPs, thus optimising the construction in terms of sealed joints and penetration points. The supporting structure, consisting of clamping plates and tensioning cables arranged on both sides of the VIP, secures the VIP in position and transfers the forces acting on the system. Variants aimed at optimising the system address aspects such as the lamination of the VIP layers, the number of fixing points, adaptability to existing structural framework conditions (lateral connections and terminations), additional moulded components to improve sealing and cable guidance. A final variant involves the use of a PTFE film instead of the cable (hogged membrane). The wall systems presented promise outstanding insulation values (U-values). These are very slim constructions, more skin-like than wall-like in character.

www.jan-cremers.com
Lit.: Cremers (2007), Applications of Vacuum Insulation Systems in the Building Envelope.

Surfaces.07
PALACIO DE CONGRESSO BADAJOZ
Selgascano, José Selgas and Lucía Cano,
Madrid

ill. Surfaces.07.1, p. 25

The external form of the 15,000 m² *Palacio de Congresos* in Badajoz in Spain is defined by a perimeter ring, 75 metres in diameter and 14 metres in height, woven of elliptical-section translucent GRP profiles, enclosing the building in a manner similar to traditional willow fencing. The envelope, formed out of a total of 12 km of profile material, illustrates the potential of composite materials. Composites, being the combination of at least two positively joined or adhesively bonded substances, display properties that are significantly optimised in comparison with their components. Lightweight structures of efficient composites such as glass-fibre-reinforced aluminium *(glare)* or carbon-fibre-reinforced plastic (CRP), which play an important role in automobile and aircraft manufacturing, are still seen as experimental forms of construction, especially in architecture. The geometry of the load-bearing cross section of the lightweight, elastic GRP profiles used here was optimised in response to the requirement to provide shade during the daytime and reflect artificial lighting in a specific way at night. The external dimensions of the conference centre reproduce the dimensions of an old bull-fighting arena which formerly occupied the site.

www.selgascano.com
www.new-composites.com

Energy.06
POWER LEAP
Elizabeth Anne Redmond,
Ann Arbor

ill. Energy.06.1, p. 34

Power Leap is a prototype flooring system that uses piezoelectric technology to convert kinetic energy induced by humans into electric energy. The system is installed in selected public and semi-public places to make use of the electric pulses generated by the steps of joggers, or dance club guests, for example. The tiles consist of sheet metal-reinforced

piezoceramic plates covered in nickel electrodes. Pressure on these plates creates a voltage that perates an LED light system within the tile.

www.elizabethredmond.net
Lit.: Priya, Inman (2008), Energy Harvesting Technologies.

Information.07
PULP-BASED COMPUTING
Marcelo Coelho and Pattie Maes,
Fluid Interface Group,
MIT Cambridge, MA

ill. Information.07.1, p. 44

Pulp-Based Computing explores the possibilities of combining paper manufacturing processes, smart materials and printing technologies. Through the controlled introduction of electronically conductive dye (conductive paste) into the fibre pulp during the manufacture of the paper, sensors and actuators can be produced which, in terms of their physical and tactile properties, look and behave like paper. The composite material can communicate digital information and can thus, for example, be used in the context of sensor-actuator systems. *Pulp-Based Computing* represents an independent conceptual approach within the ubiquitous and pervasive field of computing, in terms of both the technical feasibility of such systems and the problem of their general acceptance, which can be increased through their materialisation in paper form.

http://ambient.media.mit.edu
Lit.: Coelho, Maes et al. (2007),
Pulp-Based Computing.

Light.05
PRINTED ELECTRONICS
Oliver Wiesener,
Munich

ill. Light.05.1, p. 54

Using innovative *Printed Electronics* different electronic control elements and circuits can be combined into a singular element: a film printed with electronic functions. Owing to its low weight, its great flexibility and a thickness of only one to two millimetres, the special film allows slim, geometrically sophisticated design solutions to be devised for electrical appliances and the control elements of service engineering applications. The switching functionality of the control surfaces is based on the principle of capacitive sensor technology, so that pressure-sensitivity is individually adjustable for each controller. These can be combined with electroluminescent film to create an intuitive user interface. Used as the background for symbol keys, they produce homogeneous illumination that remains easily visible in the dark and which can be adjusted for specific keys. The *Printed Electronics* demonstrate the potential of the paint-like, printable, electrically-conductive and luminescent pastes that are currently being intensively researched and which open up new possibilities for the design of information-active surfaces and envelopes. One visionary perspective involves using membrane constructions of variable degrees of transparency with integrated printed circuits, for example in combination with energy- or light-generating surfaces.

www.schreiner-variolight.de
Lit.: Arning, Steiger (2008), Printed Electronics Elektronik, pp. 10 – 15.

structure, leading from the skeletal floor segments, also constructed of carbon, into the spherical, self-supporting dome. *R129* was preceded by various experimental studies in which construction designs of transparent domes without metallic connecting elements were investigated. The proposed bonding technology optimises the flow of forces within the segmented envelope without affecting its consistent overall appearance. The combination of different nanotechnological coatings (anti-scratch, Low-E), switchable electrochromic films for shading and unobtrusive thin-layer solar cells provides the envelope with a high degree of functionality. The floor segment conceals underfloor heating and all other service-engineering supply components. The internal partitioning does not involve any fixed installations or walls. A central module contains the bathroom facilities and the kitchen. In the remaining free area, individual zones for working and sleeping can be created by means of special functional elements (cells).

www.wernersobek.de
Lit.: Sobek, Blandini (2008), Prototype of a frameless structural glass shell, pp. 278 – 282. Sobek (2007), Entwerfen im Leichtbau, pp. 70 – 82.

R

Surfaces.08
R129
Werner Sobek, Stuttgart

ill. Surfaces.08.2, p. 12

The planned experimental construction *R129* seeks to exploit all currently available innovative means of nanotechnology, sensor technology and general material research for the design of a multifunctional, energy-efficient and structurally advanced lightweight building envelope. In terms of its objectives, it can be seen as a constructed manifesto of technology transfer. In fact, the overall appearance and details of *R129* reflect a system-integrative thinking derived from the field of lightweight construction, but one that is oriented more on solutions from automotive design and aerospace technology than the element-based constructions found in the field of building. As a flexible building that is self-sufficient in terms of energy, *R129* is designed to be used either by a single person or a group (family) for working and living. The lenticular, continuously-moulded envelope consists of a very lightweight and transparent plastic. Moulded carbon components providing lateral support around the circumference are integrated into the

Information.08
RECONFIGURABLE HOUSE
Usman Haque, Adam Somlai-Fischer, Haque Design + Research, Aether Architecture with The Reorient Team, London and Budapest

ill. Information.08.2, p. 40

The *Reconfigurable House* is a room installation consisting of numerous low-tech components which can be recombined by visitors (users) according to their own preferences. The project can be seen as a critique of the ubiquitous use of computing inherent in the concept of the Smart Home, which makes the technology as inconspicuous as possible, but in doing so deprives the user of influence and free will. According to this view, Smart Homes adapt poorly to the changing needs of their inhabitants, because they are permanently hard-wired according to strict parameters imposed by algorithms and designers. In contrast, the behaviour of the *Reconfigurable House* can be continually modified by plugging together the sensors and actuators in infinitely new configurations. It is open in every respect. By means of a simple interface, visitors can transform reactions and interactions via the software. The hardware of the house (walls and space-defining objects) consists for the most part of simple children's toys which can be freely manipulated (hacked) with even a small amount of technical knowledge. Cat Brick Wall, Mist Laser Garden,

Monkey Corridor and Radio Penguin Ceiling react to acoustic impulses, noises, light, touch and movement. The project uses open-source programming environment processing based on the open-source hardware platform Arduino. It explores interaction in a broader sense, going beyond the usual approaches of automated variety.

http://house.propositions.org.uk
www.haque.co.uk
www.aether.hu
http://lowtech.propositions.org.uk
Lit.: Haque (2006), Arquitetura, Interaçao e Sistemas. In Arquitetura & Urbanismo, pp. 68 – 71.

Surfaces.09
REFLEXBETON—BLINGCRETE
Heike Klussmann,
Studio Berlin and University of Kassel

ill. Surfaces.09.1, p. 39

The innovative material *Reflexbeton* combines the positive properties of concrete (fire safety, strength, building methods) with the properties of retroreflection. Retroreflective surfaces reflect incident rays of light (sunlight, artificial lighting) precisely in the direction of the light source. This optical phenomenon is usually created by means of glass microbeads embedded in a carrier material. The retroreflective properties are decisively influenced by the roundness and clarity of the beads as well as by the bond between the glass microbeads and the carrier material. Advantages over paints and coatings include resistance to abrasion, the inherent quality of the surface and the possibility of approval as a building product due to the concrete matrix (carrier matrix) on which it is based. The properties of *Reflexbeton* open up a wide range of design possibilities in architecture and in road safety applications. Possible applications include the durable structural safety marking of edges and danger areas (steps, curbs, railway platforms), as well as the design of structurally integrated guidance systems and innovative surface building components (façade, floor, ceiling). Because of its haptic qualities, *Reflexbeton* can also be used for tactile guide systems for the blind. Its aesthetic qualities arise from the permanent integration of the dematerialising effect of light. *Reflexbeton* represents a category of new materials with their own logic of effect which cannot readily be described in the usual terms of weight, form, construction and surface.

www.klussmann.org
www.atelierk10.de

Information.09
SENSILLAE
Chris Woebken,
New York

ill. Information.09.1, p. 48

The apparatus of the *Sensillae* design study creates the framework of an insect-human interaction using insects as biosensors. A 'sensillum' is an organ, generally consisting of a hair or pores and two sensory cells (receptors), for sensing chemical or mechanical stimuli. Considered objectively, insects are highly robust, robot-like, biological constructs that can easily be bred. In terms of the technical logic of scale, comprising macro, micro and nano, insects occupy the microtechnical dimensional level. Their size makes them suitable for use as biosensor devices. The different pieces of equipment, developed on a context-related basis, make it possible for humans to experience the sensory perceptions of an insect. Beyond its task-specific use, this interaction helps develop a deeper understanding of nature, since the insect's way of reacting is used as the basis for representing the results from the biosensory input of the *sensillae* interfaces. The *sensillae* permit a relationship of trust to evolve between insect and human, which at the same time influences people's perception of a technology that is often seen as alien.

www.woebken.net
Lit.: Featherstone (2007), Cybugs, pp. 66 – 67.

Energy.07
SILENT ENERGY
Jannis Huelsen,
Braunschweig

ill. Energy.07.1, p. 48

Silent Energy is an interactive exhibition concept. Normally, users do not actually see the consumption and generation of energy taking place as such. Gauges attached to various energy-harvesting elements display just how much energy can be harvested in an everyday environment. A micro-generator activated by depressing a door handle produces 0.2 W/s, while a turbine installed in a water tap generates 0.4 W/s. Piezoceramic elements integrated in the seating surface of a chair can generate up to 412 W/s when a person sits down. By using the exhibited objects, visitors become active energy producers.

http://jannishuelsen.com
Lit.: Priya, Inman (2008), Energy Harvesting Technologies.

Information.10
SKETCH FURNITURE
(AUGMENTED DESIGN
Front,
Stockholm

ill. Information.10.1, p. 29

The *Sketch Furniture* by the Swedish design group FRONT is created using a combination of the *Motion Capture* process, developed for film and computer animation, with *Rapid Prototype* technologies. The Motion Capture process can be understood as a variant of the concept of *Augmented Reality*. Whereas AR technology augments the real world with context-related embellishments in the form of computer-generated information which can be perceived through the senses in real time, and synchronised continuously with the movements of the eyes, the head and other sensor-linked parts of the body, *Motion Capture* registers the movements of objects and people conveyed via optical markers (which can be captured using cameras) and non-optical markers (using sensors) and transforms these into film sequences. Freehand sketches created in space can also be materialised if a pen with an optically marked tip is used. The trace of the strokes drawn in the air is transformed through Motion Capture technologies into digital 3D data sets, from which a three-dimensional model can be generated using a Rapid Prototyping method. In the variant of stereolithography chosen here, the objects are built up layer by layer from a liquid, light-hardening plastic using a laser.

www.frontdesign.se
http://fabathome.org
Lit.: Boeing (2007), 3D-Drucker für das Volk. Lipschitz (2004), Ubiquitous Computing. Lordick (2005), Mit Rapid Prototyping zu räumlichen Anamorphosen, pp. 141–150.

Energy.08
SOFT HOUSE
Kennedy & Violich Architeture,
KVA MATx,
Boston

ill. Energy.08.4, p. 38

Soft House is a project featuring a building made of prefabricated, adaptable elements with a difference: the structure can generate energy by means of photovoltaically active curtains. The textiles can be used for sun protection as well as for energy generation. The energy is harvested by strips of plastic-coated, thin film solar cells incorporated in the fabric. Up to 16 kilowatt-hours of electricity can be generated every day in this manner, which corresponds to half of the energy required each day by an average American household (US standard), or one and a half times the amount required by an average European household. The electricity generated is drawn directly from the curtains. The user can simply decide to open the curtains if the available sunlight is to be used for illumination, or to draw them if the sunlight is to be used as a source of energy.

www.kvarch.net
Lit.: Luque, Hegedus (2003), Handbook of Photovoltaic Science and Engineering.

Climate.09
SPATIUM GELATUM AND
BREEDING SPACES
Zbiegniew Oksiuta,
Cologne

ill. Climate.09.1, p. 17

The research project *Spatium Gelatum (congealed space)* combines knowledge from the fields of architecture, art and natural science with the goal of creating a biological habitat that will form a new type of spatial, energetic and ecological unit. The new system is intended, as far as possible, to be soft, biological (bioregenerative) and indeterminate. The studies relate to dynamic processes in fluids, gel solidification phenomena and phases of transition from fluid to solid material. The multiform structures and forms, up to 2.4 metres in diameter and consisting of water, biopolymers, glycerine and other biological materials, illustrate the key theme of deciphering the biological transformation of energy into form. The main building block is gelatine. This versatile biopolymer can be used to create either hard, soft, fluid, transparent, or opaque forms. It combines certain properties of concrete, glass and plastics, while being nonetheless fully reversible and edible. Flavourings and colourings expand this dimension and open up unknown areas for architecture and design. The forms of *Spatium Gelatum* are created in water, the gelatine being in a state of suspension (isopycnic system) as a fluid within fluids. The water serves as dynamic formwork for the gel-like mass. Formed and shaped from all sides, it is transformed into a bubble by means of oil, air, pressure and heat. In this way, isomorphic interiors and objects of virtually unlimited dimensions can be created. The basis of this amorphous form-shaping is the evolutionary principle associated with the pneu (liquid bubble) of the distribution of tension (bending energy) within polymeric surfaces (membranes). In a further development, *Breeding Spaces*, the constructions of the *Spatium Gelatum* are used to grow three-dimensional vegetable constructions as further possible biological habitats. In the aqueous medium, the shaping of the forms takes place as morphogenesis (a form of controlled explosion) from within, by means of expansion, growth and proliferation. Spatium Gelatum sees the future in the symbiosis of the technologies of organisms and the dry methods of human technology. It is a vision of habitats that do not stand on solid foundations but, continually reforming themselves, live on the interface of collaboration.

www.oksiuta.de
Lit.ı Oksiuta (2005), Spatium Gelatum & Breeding Spaces. Oksiuta (2007), New Biological Habitats in the Biosphere and in Space, p. 122.

Climate.10
STEMCLOUD V2.0 — THE GUADALQUIVIR EXPERIMENT
EcoLogic Studio, Claudia Pasquero and Marco Poletto, London

ill. Climate.10.2, p. 33

STEMcloud is the title of a series of experimental installations that simulate ecological processes (ecoMachines), the functioning of which is tested under exhibition conditions in direct contact and interaction with visitors. *STEMcloud v2.0* is the prototypical scaling-down of an arrangement, designed as architecture, that relates to the ecosystem of the Guadalquivir. This river, which flows through Seville, is in a critical condition. The model proposes the development and testing of an architectural prototype, functioning like an oxygen generation plant, the technological matrix of which allows the breeding of micro-organisms living in the Guadalquivir. The transparency and porosity of the architectural system make it possible to demonstrate the process. This extensive installation consists of hoses sealed with plastic caps (valves) and combined into branched bundles, which grow out of plastic containers filled with river water. Visitors are asked to stimulate the micro-organisms living in the water to produce oxygen by supplying them with nutrients and carbon dioxide (from their breath) and by regulating the lighting level, thus improving the microclimatic situation of the exhibition space. The surface tension of the containers (as an indicator of the internal pressure) and the colour and cloudiness of the water indicate the process status of STEMcloud. This becomes increasingly divergent, owing to the inconsistency of the lighting in the exhibition space, exacerbated by changing coloured artificial lighting and the low-tech character of the regulating systems at branches of the hose in the different areas of the installation. The careful arrangement of the installation creates the starting conditions for a feedback-controlled interaction of increasing complexity between the inhabitants of the STEMcloud habitat (the micro-organisms) and the visitors. During the course of the process, the latter become eco-engineers who transform the exhibition space into an experimental laboratory for climate design.

www.ecologicstudio.com

Surfaces.10
SYNTHAZARDS
Syntfarm, Andreas Schlegel and Vladimir Todorovic, Singapore

ill. Surfaces.10.2, p. 35

The *Synthazards* are recreations in model form of elemental forces which occur suddenly and with extreme vehemence, the effects of which are simulated with the aid of different algorithms and prototyping processes, laser cut-outs and CNC milling machines. The objects concentrate on the formal, morphological aspects of earthquakes, drought, hurricanes, lightning, volcanic eruptions, lava flows, tsunamis and tornadoes. When humans are affected by these forces, we speak of natural catastrophes. The *Synthazards* critically reflect the relation between mankind and its environment, which is increasingly influenced by natural hazards. At the same time this approach makes use of a very informative, primarily scientific methodology on the principle (enshrined in the laws of physics) that forces are only manifested through their effect. The *Synthazards* show natural catastrophes as transformation processes affecting the condition of surfaces. This approach generates models with their own objectivising aesthetics and structural logic which (beyond the remit of this book) do not address the relationship between material and surface in the usual sense of arriving at perfection. The idea of allowing negative forces to exert a morphological effect represents a distinct conceptual approach.

www.syntfarm.org/projects/synthazards

U

Energy.09
URBAN BATTERY
MOS,
New Haven, CT

ill. Energy.09.1, p. 37

The designers propose setting up large biogenerators along the often desolate strip malls typically found on main thoroughfares in the USA. Each of these batteries works like a vertical public garden, filtering air by means of oxygen-generating microorganisms and producing biomass. An additional building at the base of the structure provides space for community activities. The glass structure functions rather like a vertical greenhouse, with a warm interior that provides ideal conditions for the air-purifying plants. A system of turbines uses the rising hot air and produces 5,000 kWh of electricity per year. The structure is a lightweight steel construction enclosed by a glass skin. The material required is minimal and no artificial cooling is needed. This keeps the cost of such a battery relatively low. Apart from requiring a water connection, the structure is self-sufficient. *Urban Batteries* have potential in the areas of energy and environmental technology, as well as the capacity to improve the quality of urban environments.

www.mos-office.net

V

Surfaces.11
**VENUS—NATURAL CRYSTAL CHAIR
(SECOND NATURE)**
Tokujin Yoshioka,
Tokyo

ill. Surfaces.11.2, p. 49

The *Venus Chair* is grown in a tank of water enriched with a mineral solution. For this purpose, a matrix made of coarse-mesh polyester fibres defining the later form is laid in the tank. The salts accumulate on the sponge-like structure and, during a crystallisation process taking around a month, create the final materiality, structural stability and surface consistency of the chair. The process, characterised by its slowness, expands the boundaries of creative action. Here, design makes use of scientific methodology and knowledge in order to generate new objects and surfaces under laboratory-like conditions by means of physical and chemical phenomena, in which the broad dialectic between the natural and the artificial is manifested through the heightened aesthetic of a synthetic nature.

http://tokujin.com

W

Information.11
WATERRADIO
Clemens Winkler,
Halle

ill. Information.11.3, p. 19

The everyday scenario of a glass filled with water (or another liquid) accidentally being knocked over provides the inspiration for the experimental, interactive design of the *Waterradio*. Its prototypical set-up consists of a number of moisture-responsive sensors, which are distributed freely over the surface of a wooden table, without being visibly present in the material, and the microtechnically controlled components of a conventional transistor radio, with the loudspeakers serving as actuators.

It is the sensor contact with liquid which sets the radio in operation; the wood becomes, as it were, acoustically active. The relationship between sensors, water and wooden surface constitutes the channel search function (the interface) of the radio, which is identified by the user as a table. Locating and controlling the radio frequencies on the surface of the wood (which, with its grain patterns and marks of use, invites touch) by using the fingers to manipulate the film of water as it forms drops, trickles and puddles, becomes a synaesthetic experience. The *Waterradio* combines the aesthetic of the natural material with the technical capacity of a sensor-actuator system to create a unique, new synthesis of surface intelligence.

http://clemenswinkler.com

Information.12
WEATHER PATTERNS
Loop.pH,
London

ill. Information.12.1, p. 27

The Weather Patterns project, created by the designers at Loop.pH, is a permanent light installation on the façade of the York Art Gallery. The project forms part of a programme called 'York: Light' and was commissioned by York City Council. As in many other cities, the authorities are carrying out a ten-year plan of light management, with the aim of making the city more attractive generally and a safer place to be at night, which it is hoped will bring long term economic benefits, especially from tourism and a stronger *evening economy*, as well as improved night time security. The York Art Gallery is a listed building in the Italian Renaissance style. The designers made use of the existing architecture by fitting five blank window recesses on the first floor of the façade with weatherproof light panels. The electroluminescence panels, which are printed with floral motifs, reflect sunlight during the day and radiate artificial light to the exterior at night, as determined by a special control system. The luminous areas communicate the weather of the day gone by in an abstract manner, using data supplied by a weather station located on the premises. With this installation, the designers also allude to the exploration of human impact on climate: in contrast to the high degree of abstraction of scientific findings, the light installation displays a direct reaction to the day's weather. The decoratively printed electroluminescence films are sandwiched between a mirror and toughened glass. A single window element is made up of two prints, each 90 × 100 cm, with a segmented pattern controlled by 8 or 16 channels. Instead of the classic dot-matrix display, the light animation has a specially created spiral-shaped pattern, which is able to reproduce basic movement, rotation and growth patterns without the pixelated aesthetic of lower resolution displays. The design was inspired by natural structures, such as sunflowers or pinecones, that grow in spirals according to a mathematical proportion. Although only five windows are illuminated, the light installation makes the large museum façade appear to dance at night.

www.loop.ph

Lit.: Arning, Steiger (2008), Printed Electronics Elektronik, pp. 10 – 15.

LITERATURE

•3deluxe (2009), Transdisciplinary Approaches to Design, Berlin, London: Frame Publishers •ACADIA 08 (2008), Silicon + Skin: Biological Processes and Computation, Proceedings of the 28th Annual Conference of the Association for Computer Aided Design in Architecture, ed. by Andrew Kudless, Neri Oxman and Marc Swackhamer • Ahmad, Maha; Bontemps, André; Sallée, Hébert; Quenard, Daniel (2006), Thermal testing and numerical simulation of a prototype cell using light wallboards coupling vacuum isolation panels and phase change material. In Energy and Buildings 38, pp. 673 – 681 • Anderson, Alison; Petersen, Alan; Wilkinson, Clare (2009), Nanotechnology, Risk and Communication, Hampshire: Palgrave • Arning, Volker; Steiger, Jürgen (2008), Antennas off the Roll —Printed Electronics. In Elements, Science Newsletter 24/ 2008, ed. by Evonik Degussa GmbH, pp. 10 – 15 • Artopoulos, Giorgos; Roudavski, Stanislav (in alphabetical order) with François Penz (2006), Adaptive Generative Patterns. In Proceedings of The Second International Conference of the Arab Society for Computer Aided Architectural Design (ASCAAD 2006), ed. by Jamal Al-Qawasmi and Zaki Mallasi (Sharjah: The Arab Society for Computer Aided Architectural Design ASCAAD, 2006), pp. 341 – 362 • Asut Bulletin 4 (2007), Interview mit F. Mattern—Reale and virtuelle Welten verschmelzen, pp. 22 – 24 • Banzi, Massimo (2008), Getting started with Arduino, Sebastopol, Cal.: O´Reilly 2008 • Barthes, Roland (1964), Mythen des Alltags [Mythologies], Frankfurt am Main: Suhrkamp 1964, pp. 79 – 81 • Baudrillard, Jean (1968), Das System der Dinge, Über unser Verhältnis zu den alltäglichen Gegenständen [System of Objects], Frankfurt am Main: Suhrkamp 1991, pp. 50 – 52 • Bechthold, Martin (2008), Innovative Surface Structures: Technology and Applications, New York: Taylor & Francis • Beesley, Philip; Bonnemaison, Sarah (2008), On Growth and Form, Organic Architecture and Beyond, Halifax: Tuns Press and Riverside Architectural Press • Benthien, Claudia (2001), Haut. Literaturgeschichte—Körperbilder—Grenzdiskurse, Reinbek bei Hamburg: Rowohlt • Berjansky, Stuart (2004), Hello DALI, Plant Services, May 2004, www.plantservices.com/articles/2004/110.html, downloaded on 20. April 2009 • BINE (Ed.) (2007), Thermoaktive Bauteilsysteme, Themeninfo I/2007, Fachinformationsdienst Karlsruhe, Büro Bonn • Building Integrated Photovoltaics BIPV (2009), www.bipv.ch/definizione_d.asp, downloaded on April 26th, 2009 • Bundesministerium für Bildung and Forschung, Deutschland BMBF (Ed.)(2005) Mikrosystemtechnik-Kongress 2005, 10th–12th October 2005 in Freiburg, published by Margret Schneider, Berlin: VDE • Bocquet, Lyderic; Duez, Cyrill; Ybert, Christophe; Clanet, Christophe (2007), Making a splash with water repellency, Nature Physics, Vol. 3, March 2007, pp. 80 – 183 • BodyNets 08 (2008), Proceedings of the ICST 3rd International Conference on Body Area Networks, ed. by the Institute for Computer Science and Telecommunications Engineering ICST, Brussels • Boeing, Niels (2006), Die Notwendigkeit einer offenen Nanotechnik. In Nanotechnologien im Kontext: Philosophische, ethische and gesellschaftliche Perspektiven, ed. by Alfred Nordmann, Joachim Schummer, Astrid Schwarz, Berlin: Akademische Verlagsgesellschaft, pp. 277 – 291 • Boeing, Niels (2007), 3D-Drucker für das Volk. Vortrag auf der Rethinking Business Conference #2, Essen, June 22nd, 2007. www.z-punkt.de/index.php?id=587, downloaded on April 24th, 2009 • Bommel, Wout van; Beld, Gerrit van den (2001), Industrial Lighting, Productivity, Health and Well-Being. In Ingineria Iluminatului—Lighting Engineering Review, Year III, Issue 7—June 2001, pp. 5 – 28 • Botthof, Alfons; Pelka, Joachim (Ed.) (2003), Mikrosystemtechnik—Zukunftsszenarien, Berlin: Springer • Broad, William J. (2005), A Web of Sensors, Taking Earth's Pulse, New York Times, May 10, 2005 • Brütting, Wolfgang; Rieß, Walter (2008), Grundlagen organischer Halbleiter, Physik-Journal 7, Nr. 5, pp. 33 – 38 • Campo, Matias del; Manninger, Sandra (2008), Speculations on Tissue Engineering and Architecture. In Silicon + Skin: Biological Processes and Computation. Proceedings of the 28th Annual Conference of the Association for Computer Aided Design in Architecture, ed. by Andrew Kudless, Neri Oxman and Marc Swackhamer, pp. 82 – 87 • Çelik, Zeynep (2006), Kinaesthesia. In Sensorium—Embodied Experience, Technology and Contemporary Art, ed. by Caroline A. Jones, Cambridge, Mass; London: MIT Press, pp. 159 – 162 • Clarke, Arthur C. (1968), 2001 A Space Odyssey, Reprint 2008, London: Orbit • Clute, John (2001), Appleseed, London: Orbit • Clyne, Manfred E.; Kline, Nathan pp. (1960), Cyborgs and Space, Astronautics, Nr. 26/27, Sept. 1960, pp. 74 – 75 • Coelho, Marcelo; Maes, Pattie; Hall, Lyndl; Berzowska, Joanna (2007), Pulp-Based Computing, A Framework for Building Computers Out of Paper. In The 9th International Conference on Ubiquitous Computing (Ubicomp 2007), Innsbruck, Austria, September 2007 • Conrad, James M. (2005), Stiquito Controlled! Making a Truly Autonomous Robot, Hoboken: Wiley-IEEE Press • Craig, William C. (2003), Zigbee: Wireless Control that Simply Works, www.zigbee.org/LeranMore/WhitePapers/tabid/257/Default.aspx, downloaded on April 26th, 2009 • Cremers, Jan (2007), Einsatzmöglichkeiten von Vakuum-Dämmsystemen im Bereich der Gebäudehülle: Technologische, bauphysikalische and architektonische Aspekte, München: Meidenbauer • Cruz, Marcos; Pike, Steve (Ed.) (2008), Neoplasmatic Design, AD Architectural Design, Vol. 78, Nr. 6, London • DALI Activity Group (2001), DALI Manual, Frankfurt, Munich: Richard Plaum • Debord, Guy (1967), Gesellschaft des Spektakels, 1st edition 1996, Berlin: Klaus Bitterman • Dauberschmidt, Christoph; Sodeikat, Christian; Schießl, Peter; Gehlen, Christoph (2008), Monitoring von Verkehrsbauten: Kontinuierliche Zustandserfassung, Sicherstellung der Dauerhaftigkeit, Tiefbau 3/2008, pp. 135—141 • Davies, Mike (1990), Eine Wand für alle Jahreszeiten: Die intelligente Umwelt erschaffen, Archplus 14, pp. 49 • Drexler, K. Eric (1986), Engines of Creation: The Coming Era of Nanotechnology. New York: Anchor Books • Eicker, Ursula (2001), Solare Technologien für Gebäude, Wiesbaden: Vieweg + Teubner • Eisenhart, Peter; Kurth, Dan; Stiehl, Horst (1995), Wie Neues entsteht: Die Wissenschaft des Komplexen and Fraktalen, Reinbek bei Hamburg: Rowohlt • Engelsmann, Stefan (2004), Neue Hüllen, bitte! In Materialwechsel—Neue Wege im Design durch funktionelle Surfaces, Tagungsband 2. Innovationsforum Oberflächentechnik & Design im DAZ Berlin, October 21st, 2004, pup. by EFDS e. V. with BTU Cottbus and the Bund Dt. Architekten BDA • Erlhoff, Michael; Marshall, Tim (2007), Design Dictionary: Perspectives on Design Terminology, ed. by the Board of International Research in Design BIRD. Basel, Boston, Berlin: Birkhäuser • Featherstone, Steve (2007), Cybugs, Cabinet 25, New York, pp. 66 – 67 • Federal Ministery of Technology and Research (Ed.) (2002), Optical Technology Made in Germany. Engl. Summary of Förderprogramm Optische Technologien, pub. by Bundesministerium für Bildung und Forschung BMBF, dated: February 2002, Bonn • Federal Office for Information Security (2004), Security Aspects and Prospective Applications of RFID-Systems, http://www.bsi.de/english/publications/studies/rfid/RIKCHA_englisch_Layout.pdf, downloaded on April 29th, 2009 • Feuerstein, Günther (2000), Cell and Capsule. Talk given at the BTU Cottbus in June 2000, authorised transcript available at www.smart-surfaces.de • FIDU eine neue Verarbeitungsmethode im Blech (2009), Blow up Pavillon 2007. www.blech.arch.ethz.ch/Main/FIDU2, downloaded on April 24th, 2009 • Finckh, Sebastian (2004), Surfaces semantisch/funktional. In Materialwechsel—Neue Wege im Design durch funktionelle Surfaces, conference proceedings 2. Innovationsforum Oberflächentechnik & Design im DAZ Berlin, Oktober 21st, 2004, pub. by EFDS e. V. with BTU Cottbus and Bund Dt. Architekten BDA • Finkenzeller, Klaus (2006), RFID-Handbook: Fundamentals and Applications in Contactless Smart Cards and Identification, Hoboken: Wiley & Sons • Fitzwilly, Egbert (2009), Simple Algae Home CO_2 Scrubber—Part 1 and 2, www.instructables.com/id/Simple_Algae_Home_CO2_Scrubber_Part_1/.pdf, downloaded on April 24th, 2009 • Fitzwilly, Egbert (2009), Make a Microbial Fuel Cell (MFC)—Part 1, www.instructables.com/id/Simple-Algae-Home-CO2-Scrubber-Part-III-An-Algae/.pdf, downloaded on April 24th, 2009 • Flusser, Vilém (1994), Gesten: Versuch einer Phänomenologie, Frankfurt: Fischer • Form + Zweck 22 (2008), Tangibility of the Digital—Die Fühlbarkeit des Digitalen, Berlin • Foucault, Michel (1966), Die Heterotopien—Der utopische Körper: Zwei Radiovorträge, zweisprachige Ausgabe, Dt.-Französ., Nachw. v. Daniel Defert, Frankfurt: Suhrkamp 2005 • Fox, Michael A. (2002), Beyond Kinetic, http://robotecture.com/Papers/papers.html, downloaded on April 26th, 2009 • Fricke, Helmut (2005), From Dewars to VIPs—One Century of Progress in Vacuum Insulation Technology. In Proceedings of the 7th International Vacuum Insulation Symposium 2005, ed. by Mark Zimmermann, Empa, Duebendorf/Zurich, Switzerland. September 28-29, pp. 5 – 14 • Fuller, Buckminster R. (1963), Operating Manual for Spaceship Earth, Baden: Lars Müller Publishers, 1 ed. 2008 • Galison, Peter (2006), Nanofacture. In Sensorium—Embodied Experience, Technology and Contemporary Art, ed. by Caroline A. Jones, Cambridge, Mass; London: MIT Press, pp. 171 – 173 • Gibson, William (1984), Neuromancer, Paperback Edition 1995, London: Voyager • Goetzberger, Adolf; Hoffmann, Volker U. (2005), Photovoltaic Solar Energy Generation, Berlin: Springer • Gold, Peter (1998), Philosophische Aspekte künstlicher Intelligenz. In Der Mensch in der Perspektive der Kognitionswissenschaften, ed. by Peter Gold and Andreas K. Engel, Frankfurt am Main: Suhrkamp, pp. 49 – 97 • Gombert, Andreas; Niggemann, Michael (2006), Organische Solarzellen für neuartige Anwendungen, www.ise.fraunhofer.de/veroeffentlichungen/infomaterial/broschuren-and-produktinformationen/alternative-photovoltaik-technologien/organische-solarzellen-fur-neuartige-anwendungen, downloaded on April 26th, 2009 • Guallarte, Vicente (Ed.) (2005), Media House Project: The House Is The Computer The Structure The Network, Barcelona, New York: Actar • Granel, Edna; Turner, Jefferon T. (2006), Ecology of Harmful Algae, Berlin: Springer • Gray, Chris Hables; Mentor, Steven; Figuroa-Sarriera, Heidi J. (Ed.) (1995), The Cyborg Handbook, London: Routledge • Green, Martin A. (2003), Third Generation Photovoltaics: Advanced Solar Energy Conversion, Berlin: Springer • Green, Martin A. (2000), Power to the People: Sunlight to Electricity Using Solar Cells, Sidney: UNSW Press • Grinewitschus, Viktor (2007), Vernetzung optimieren: InHaus2, ElectronicHome Jahrbuch, pp. 159 – 161 • Hamakawa, Yoshihiro (2004), Thin-film Solar Cells: Next Generation Photovoltaics and its Applications, Berlin: Springer • Han, Jefferson Y. (2005), Low-Cost Multi-Touch Sensing through Frustrated Total Internal Reflection. In Proceedings of the 18th Annual ACM Symposium on User Interface Software and Technology, pp. 115 – 118 • Haque, Usman (2006), Arquitetura, Interaçao e Sistemas Arquitetura & Urbanismo, AU149, Brazil, pp. 68 – 71 • Haque, Usman; Somlai-Fischer, Adam (2005), Low Tech Sensors and Actuators for Artist and Architects, http://lowtech.propositions.org.uk/, downloaded on April 26th, 2009 • Hausladen, Gerhard; Liedl, Petra; Saldanha, Michael de (2008), Climate Skin: Concepts for Building Skins That Can Do More With Less Energy, Basel: Birkhäuser • Hayes, Robert A.; Feenstra, B. Johan (2003), Video-speed electronic paper based on electrowetting, Nature 425, pp. 383 – 385 • Heckman, Davin (2008), A Small World: Smart Houses and the Dream of the Perfect Day, Durham and London: Duke University Press • Henriksson, Marielle; Berglund, Lars A.; Lindström, Tom; Nishino, Takashi (2008), Cellulose Nanopaper Structures of High Toughness, Biomacromolecules, Vol. 9, No. 6, 2008, pp. 1579 – 1585 • Herlitze, Lothar (2004), Moderne Low-E-Verglasungen. In Materialwechsel—Neue Wege im Design durch funktionelle Surfaces, Tagungsband 2. Innovationsforum Oberflächentechnik & Design im DAZ Berlin, October 21st 2004, pub. by EFDS e. V. with BTU Cottbus and the Bund Dt. Architekten BDA • Hillmer, Hartmut et al. (2008), Sun Glasses for Buildings based on Micro Mirror Arrays: Technology, Control by Networked H Hamakawa, Yoshihiro (2004), Thin-film Solar Cells: Next Generation Photovoltaics and its Applications, Berlin: Springer • Hochman, Paul (2009), How Green is Wireless Electricity? Fast Company, Issue 132 February 2009 • Hochman, Paul (2009), Wireless Electricity is here (Seriously), Fast Company, Issue 132 February 2009 • Hodge, Brooke (2006), Skin + Bones: Parallel Practices in Fashion and Architecture, London: Thames & Hudson • Hoppe, Ronald H. W. (2004), Thermogeneratoren and Kühlung für leistungselektronische Anwendungen, www.presse.uni-augsburg.de/unipressedienst/2004/pm2004_004.shtml, downloaded on April 26th, 2009 • Hornecker, Eva; Buur, Jacob (2006), Getting a Grip on Tangible Interaction: A Framework on Physical Space and Social Interaction. In Designing for Tangible Interactions, CHI 2006 Proceedings, April 22 – 27, 2006, Montréal, Québec, Canada, pp. 437 – 446 •

House_n Research Consortium (2005), Research Topics, MIT Cambridge, Mass., October, 15, 2005, http://architecture.mit.edu/house_n/publications.html, downloaded on April 26th, 2009
• Igoe, Tom (2006), Sensor Interfaces. Make: technology on your time, Vol. 05, Februar 2006, p.161
• Informationsforum RFID e. V. (pub.) (2007), Basiswissen RFID, Berlin, 2nd edition, pp.5–14
• Jones, Richard A. L. (2007), Soft Machines: Nanotechnology and Life, Oxford University Press 2004, Paperback 2007
• Jun'ichiro, Tanizaki (1987), Lob des Schattens: Entwurf einer japanischen Ästhetik [In Praise of Shadows], Zürich: Manesse
• Kaltenbach, Frank (2005), PCM-Latentwärmespeicher—Heizen and Kühlen ohne Energieverbrauch? PCM Latent Thermal-Storage Media—Heating and Cooling without Energy Consumption? Detail 6/2005, pp.660–665
• Karl, Jürgen (2006), Dezentrale Energiesysteme: Neue Technologien im liberalisierten Energiemarkt, München: Oldenbourg Wissenschaftsverlag
• Kelly, Richard (1952), Lighting As An Integral Part of Architecture, College Art Journal, Vol. XII
• Kerckhove, Derrick de (2001), The Architecture of Intelligence (IT Revolution in Architecture). Basel: Birkhäuser
• Klooster, Thorsten (2005), Funktionelle Surfaces im Bauwesen. Forum der Forschung 18/2005. pp.103–106
• Knodt, Reinhard (1994), Ästhetische Korrespondenzen, Stuttgart: Reclam
• Könches, Barbara; Weibel, Peter (Ed.) (2005), unSICHTBARes. Kunst_Wissenschaft: Algorithmen als Schnittstellen zwischen Kunst and Wissenschaft, Internationaler Mediekunstpreis 2004, Bern: Benteli
• Kraft, Sabine; Müller, Agnes Katharina (2007), Kennziffern zum Energieverbrauch, Archplus 184, pp.32–33
• Kranenburg, Rob van (2008), The Internet of Things: A critique of ambient technology and the all-seeing network of RFID, Report prepared by Rob van Kranenburg for the Institute of Network Cultures with contributions by Sean Dodson, Amsterdam: Network02 Notebooks, www.networkcultures.org/networknotebooks, downloaded on April 26th, 2009
• Kreith, Frank; Goswami, D. Yogi (2007), Handbook of Energy Efficiency and Renewable Energy, Boca Raton: CRC Press
• Kubrick, Johanna; Kim, Ji-Hun; Kösch, Sascha (2008), Kluge Dinge: Das neue Netz, De:Bug 127
• Küster, Harald (2004), Surfaces für Tages- and Kunstlicht. In Materialwechsel—Neue Wege im Design durch funktionelle Surfaces, conference proceedings 2. Innovationsforum Oberflächentechnik & Design im DAZ Berlin, October 21st, 2004, pub. by EFDS e. V. with BTU Cottbus and the Bund Dt. Architekten BDA
• Kunze, Christophe; Holtmann, Carsten; Schmidt, Andreas; Stork, Wilhelm (2008), Kontextsensitive Technologien and Intelligente Sensorik für Ambient-Assisted-Living-Anwendungen, 1. Deutscher Kongress Ambient Assisted Living (AAL 08), Berlin, www.fzi.de/ipe/eng/publikationen.php?id=1967, downloaded on April 26th, 2009
• Lem, Stanislav (1961), Solaris, First Harvest Edition 1987, New York: Harcourt
• Lipp, Lauritz L. (2004), Interaktion zwischen Mensch and Computer im Ubiquitious Computing, Münster: Lit-Verlag
• Lin, Shawn-Yu (2008), A vertically aligned carbon nanotube array: the darkest manmade material, Nano Letters 8, p.446
• Lindinger, Manfred (2008), Casimir-Effekt: Spielball einer seltsamen Kraft, F.A.Z. No. 25, 30.01.2008, p.N2
• Lowgren, Jonas (2009), Interaction Design, www.interactiondesign.org/encyclopedia/interaction_design.html, downloaded on April 26th, 2009
• Lordick, Daniel (2005), Schiefe Bilder—Mit Rapid Prototyping zu räumlichen Anamorphosen, conference proceedings of the DgfGG, (Universität Hannover 2005), pp.141–150
• Lüling, Claudia (Ed.) (2000), Architektur unter Strom: Photovoltaik gestalten, Berlin: TU Berlin
• Luque, Antonio; Hegedus, Steven (Ed.) (2003), Handbook of Photovoltaic Science and Engineering, Hoboken: Wiley & Sons
• Luinge, Henk J.; Veltink, Peter H. (2005), Measuring Orientation of Human Body Segments using Gyroscopes and Accelerometers, Medical and Biological Engineering and Computing Vol. 43, Number 2, pp.273–282
• Lstiburek, Joseph W. (2007), The Perfect Wall, ASHREA Journal, vol. 49, no. 5, pp.74–78
• Maeda, John (2006), Simplicity—the Art of Complexity. In Simplicity—the Art of Complexity, ed. by Gerfried Stocker and Christine Schöpf, Ostfildern: Hatje Cantz, pp.14–15 (Engl.), pp.16–17 (Dt.)
• Manzini, Ezio (1989), The Material of Invention: Material and Design, London: The Design Council
• Markvart, Tom; Castañer, Luis (2003), Practical handbook of photovoltaics: fundamentals and applications, New York: Elsevier Science
• Markvart, Tom (Ed.) (2000), Solar Electricity, Hoboken: John Wiley & Sons
• Mau, Bruce; Leonhard, Jennifer; Institute without Boundaries (Ed.) (2004), Massive Change, New York: Phaidon 2004
• Mazé, Ramia (2007), Occupying Time: Design, Technology, and the Form of Interaction, Stockholm: Axl Books
• Mertins, Detlef (2004), Where Architecture meets Biology: An Interview with Detlef Mertins. Interact or Die!, ed. by Joke Brouwer and Arjen Mulder, Rotterdam: V2 Publishing, pp.110–131
• Metzner, Christoph (2004), Transparente and farbige Kratzschutzschichten. In Materialwechsel—Neue Wege im Design durch funktionelle Surfaces, conference proceedings 2. Innovationsforum Oberflächentechnik & Design im DAZ Berlin, October 21st, 2004, pub. by EFDS e. V. with BTU Cottbus and the Bund Dt. Architekten BDA
• Meyer, Frederic; Bögel, Gerd vom; Ressel, Christian; Dimitrov, Todor (2008), inHaus2: Intelligent construction site logistics. In RFID SysTech 2008, 4th European Workshop on RFID Systems and Technologies, ed. by T. Hollstein, June, 10–11, 2008 in Freiburg, Germany, Berlin: VDE-Verlag
• Mignonneau, Laurent; Sommerer, Christa (2003), Von der Poesie des Programmierens zur Forschung als Kunstform, publiziert auf netzspannung.org am 2. December 2004, http://netzspannung.org/positions/digital-transformations, downloaded on April 26th, 2009
• Mills, Jonathan W. (1992), Stiquito: A Small, Simple, Inexpensive Hexapod Robot, Technical Report TR363a. www.cs.indiana.edu/cgi-bin/techreports/TRNNN.cgi?trnum=TR363a, downloaded on April 24th, 2009
• Moggridge, Bill (2006), Designing Interactions. Cambridge, Mass.: MIT Press
• Munday, Jeremy N.; Capasso, Federico; Parsegian, V. Adrian (2008), Measured long-range repulsive Casimir—Lifshitz forces, Nature 457, (2008), pp.170–173
• Nachtigall, Werner (2002), Bionik: Grundlagen and Beispiele für Ingenieure and Naturwissenschaftler. Berlin: Springer Verlag
• Nakaya, Fujiko (1972), The Making of „Fog" or Low-Hanging Stratus Cloud. In Pavilion: Experiments in Art and Technology, ed. by Billy Klüver, Julie Martin and Barbara Rose, New York: E. P. Dutton, pp.207–224
• Neudeck, Andreas; Thurner, Frank (2008), Leuchtende Verbindungen. Design-Report 03/2008
• Nordmann, Alfred (2007), Schöne, neue Nanowelt, Alfred Nordmann im Interview mit Niels Boeing, ZEIT 47/2007, p.41
• Nordmann, Alfred (2006), Unsichtbare Ursprünge: Herbert Gleiter and der Beitrag der Materialwissenschaft. In Nanotechnologien im Kontext: Philosophische, ethische and gesellschaftliche Perspektiven, ed. by Alfred Nordmann, Joachim Schummer, Astrid Schwarz, Berlin: Akademische Verlagsgesellschaft, pp.81–96
• Oksiuta, Zbigniew (2004), Spatium Gelatum & Breeding Spaces, Architektur Biennale Venedig and Archilab Orleans 2004. Köln: Walther König
• Oksiuta, Zbigniew (2007), New Biological Habitats in the Biosphere and in Space, Leonardo, Vol. 40, No. 2, p.122
• Oosterhuis, Kas (2002), We build spaceships, Metropolis Magazine, 01/2002
• Pallasmaa, Juhani (2008), The Eyes of the Skin: Architecture and the Senses, Hoboken: Wiley & Sons
• Pawlowski, Robert (2006), Adaptive Dachtragwerke: Entwicklung eines Entwurfsverfahrens, Betrachtung ausgewählter Aspekte, Dissertation TU München, July 10th, 2006
• Pearce, John (1972), An Architect´s view. In Pavilion: Experiments in Art and Technology, ed. by Billy Klüver, Julie Martin and Barbara Rose, New York: E. P. Dutton, pp.255–65
• Penone, Giuseppe (1969), Den Wald wiederholen. In Giuseppe Penone: Die Adern des Steins, Ausst.-Kat. Kunstmuseum Bonn 1997, pp.83–109
• Platt, Charles (2006), My Love Affair with LEDs, Make: technology on your time, Vol. 08, p.133
• Priya, Shashank; Inman, Daniel J. (Eds.) (2008), Energy Harvesting Technologies, New York: Springer
• Pushparaj, Victor L. et al. (2007), Flexible energy storage devices based on nanocomposite paper, PNAS August 21st, 2007, Vol. 104, No. 34, pp.13574–13577
• Quaschning, Volker (2008), Erneuerbare Energien and Klimaschutz: Hintergründe- Techniken Anlagenplanung Wirtschaftlichkeit, München: Hanser Verlag
• Raymond, Eric S. (2001), The Cathedral & the Bazaar: Musings on Linux and Open Source by an Accidental Revolutionary, Sebastopol, Cal.: O´Reilly
• Rea, Mark S. (2002), Light—Much more than Vision. In Light and Human Health: EPRI/LRO 5th International Lighting Research Symposium, Palo Alto, CA: The Lighting Research Office of the Electric Power Research Institute, pp.1–15
• Reichholf, Josef H. (2008), Stabile Ungleichgewichte: Die Ökologie der Zukunft, Frankfurt: Suhrkamp
• Richmond, Amos (Ed.) (2004), Handbook of Microalgal Culture, Oxford: Blackwell Science
• Rindelhardt, Udo (2001), Photovoltaische Stromversorgung, Wiesbaden: Vieweg+Teubner
• Rötzer, Florian (1997), Virtueller Raum oder Weltraum? Raumutopien des digitalen Zeitalters. In Mythos Internet, ed. by Stefan Münker and Alexander Roesler, Frankfurt: Suhrkamp, pp.368–389
• Ris, Hans Rudolf (2008), Beleuchtungstechnik für Praktiker, 4th edition, Berlin: VDE
• Rosol, Christoph (2007), RFID: Vom Ursprung einer allgegenwärtigen Kulturtechnologie, Berlin: Kadmos
• Saffer, Dan (2009), Designing Gestural Interfaces, Sebastopol, Cal.: O´Reilly
• Schievelbusch, Wolfgang (1983), Lichtblicke: Zur Geschichte der künstlichen Helligkeit im 19. Jahrhundert, München and Wien: Hanser
• Schmidt, Anne; Fontenot, Anthony; Rosenzweig, Jakob (2007), Nueva Orleans al descubierto (Exposing New Orleans), Neutra, NTRES S.C., Sevilla, September 2007, pp.38–45
• Schmidt, Jürgen (1995), Transparente Wärmedämmung in der Architektur: Materialien—Technologie—Anwendung, Heidelberg: Müller
• Schubert, Karsten (2008), Das Potenzial des Lastmanagements als Ersatz für Regelenergiekraftwerke bei einem steigenden Anteil erneuerbarer Energieträger, München: GRIN
• Schwarz, Astrid. E. (2008), Grüne Nanotechnologie? In Nanobiotechnologien: Philosophische, anthropologische and ethische Fragen, ed. by Georg Hofmeister, Kristian Köchy, Martin Norwig, Freiburg: Alber (forthcoming)
• Scott, Felicity D. (2007), Architecture or Techno-utopia: Politics after Modernism, Cambridge, Mass.: MIT Press
• Sekitani, Tsuyoshi; Noguchi, Yoshiaki; Hata, Kenji; Fukushima, Takanori; Aida, Takuzo; Someya, Takao (2008), A Rubberlike Stretchable Active Matrix Using Elastic Conductors, Science 12, Vol. 321, No. 5895, pp.1468–1472
• Seymour, Sabine (2009), Fashionable Technology: The Intersection of Design, Fashion, Science and Technology, Wien: Springer
• Gleiniger, Andreas; Vrachliotis, Georg (Ed.) (2008), Simulation—Präsentationstechnik and Erkenntnisinstrument, Basel: Birkhäuser
• Sommer, Adolf W. (2008), Passivhäuser: Planung—Konstruktion—Details—Beispiele, Köln: Rudolf Müller
• Siegert, Lothar (2004), PVD-Beschichtungen als Gestaltungselement. In Materialwechsel—Neue Wege im Design durch funktionelle Surfaces, conference proceedings 2. Innovationsforum Oberflächentechnik & Design im DAZ Berlin, October 21st, 2004, pub. by EFDS e. V. with BTU Cottbus and the Bund Dt. Architekten BDA
• Sinclair Eakin, Julie (2007), A Gleam in the Eye: China makes room for an energy-efficient media-wall, ID Magazine 54/1, pp.47–48
• Sobek, Werner (2007), Entwerfen im Leichtbau, Themenheft Forschung 3, ed. by Universität Stuttgart, pp.70–82
• Sobek, Werner; Blandini, Lucio (2008), Prototype of a frameless structural glass shell, Structural Engineering International, Vol. 18, No. 3, pp.278–282
• Sørensen, Bent (2004), Renewable energy: its physics, engineering, use, environmental impacts, economy, and planning aspects, 3 ed., Burlington, Mass.: Academic Press
• Spinoff (1992), Reflective Insulation. In Spinoff 1992, ed. by James J. Haggerty National Aeronautics and Space Administration NASA, Office of Commercial Programs, Technology Transfer Division, p.75
• Stadt Zürich (pub.) (2004), Plan Lumière Zürich: Gesamtkonzept 1. April 2004, www.stadt-zuerich.ch/content/hbd/de/index/staedtebau_u_planung/plan_lumiere/plan_lumiere_gesamtkonzept.html, downloaded on April 26th, 2009
• Stallmann, Richard (2007), Why "Open Source" misses the point of Free Software, www.gnu.org/philosophy/open-source-misses-the-point.html, downloaded on April 26th, 2009
• Steed, Jonathan W.; Turner, David R.; Wallace, Karl (2007), Cor Concepts in Supramolecular Chemistry and Nanochemistry: From Supramolecules to Nanotechnology, Chichester: Wiley & Sons
• Stephenson, Neal (1995), The Diamond Age, or, A Young Lady's Illustrated Primer, New York: Bantam Books
• Sterling, Bruce (2005), Shaping Things, Cambridge, Mass.: MIT Press
• Storch, Maja; Cantieni, Benita; Hüther, Gerald; Tschacher, Wolfgang (2006), Embodiment: Die Wechselwirkung von Körper and Psyche verstehen und nutzen, Bern: Huber
• Storrs Hall, John (1996), Utility Fog: The Stuff that Dreams Are Made Of. In Nanotechnology: Molecular Speculations on Global Abundance, ed. by B. C. Crandall, Cambridge, Mass.: MIT Press, pp.161–184
• Tauschek, Stefan (2007), Von Mikromaschinen and Siliziumkreiseln. Monolithische Gyroskope erobern die Consumerindustrie, Technology Transfer 2, October 2007, pp.2–4
• Telhan, Orkan (2007), Social Sensing and its Display, S.M. Thesis, Cambridge, Mass.: MIT
• Tenpierik, Martin; Cauberg, Hans (2006), Vacuum Insulation Panel: friend or foe? In Proceedings PLEA2006—The 23rd Conference on Passive and Low Energy Architecture, Geneva, Switzerland, 6-8 September 2006. pp.6–8
• Teuffel, Patrick (2004), Entwerfen adaptiver Strukturen: Lastpfadmanagement zur Optimierung tragender Leichtbaustrukturen, Dissertation ILEK, Universität Stuttgart, p.12
• Thackara, John (2005), In the Bubble: Designing in a Complex World, Cambridge, Mass.: MIT Press
• The Economist (2007), Illumination—Everlasting Light: An environmentally friendly bulb that may never need changing, June 19th, 2007
• Turner, Andrew (2007), RoboHouse, Make: technology on your time, Vol. 10, May 2007, pp.72–75
• Ullmer, Brygg Anders (2002), Tangible Interfaces for Manipulating Aggregates of Digital Information, Doctoral Dissertation, Cambridge, Mass.: MIT Media Lab
• Ullmer, Brygg Anders; Ishii, Hiroshi (2001), Emerging Frameworks for Tangible User Interfaces. In Human-Computer Interaction in the New Millenium, ed. by John M. Carroll, New York: Addison-Wesley, pp.579–601
• Umweltbundesamt (pub.) (2009), Beleuchtungstechnik mit geringerer Umweltbelastung, 3rd edition, March 18th, 2009, www.umweltbundesamt.de/energie/archiv/UBA_Light_Ausgabe_03.pdf, downloaded on April 26th, 2009
• Vollen, Jason; Laver, Jed; Clifford, Dale (2008), High Performance Masonry Wall Systems: principles derived from natural analogues. In Deep Matters: The 2008 ACSA/AIA Teachers Seminar, https://www.acsa-arch.org/files/conferences/teachers/2008/cliffordlavervollen.pdf, downloaded on April 24th, 2009
• Wagemann, Hans-Günther; Eschrich, Heinz (2007), Photovoltaik: Solarstrahlung and Halbleitereigenschaften, Solarzellenkonzepte and Aufgaben, Wiesbaden: Vieweg + Teubner
• Wahrig (2006), Deutsches Wörterbuch, München: Bertelsmann Lexikon Institut, 7th edition
• Wang, Zhong Lin; Dai, Liming; Qu, Liangti; Stone, Morley; Xia, Zhenhai; (2008), Carbon Nanotube Arrays with Strong Shear Binding-On and Easy Normal Lifting-Off, Science 10, Vol. 322, No. 5899, pp.238–242
• Warneke, Brett; Last, Matt; Liebowitz, Brian; Pister, Kristofer S. J. (2001), Smart Dust: Communicating with a Cubic-Millimeter Computer, Computer, Vol. 34, January 2001, pp.2–9
• Weinläder, Helmut; Ebert, Hans-Peter; Fricke, Jochen (2005), VIG Vacuum Insulation Glass. In Proceedings of the 7th International Vacuum Insulation Symposium, ed. by Mark Zimmermann, Empa, Duebendorf/Zurich, Switzerland. September 28-29, 2005. pp.197–204
• Weiser, Mark (1991), The Computer for the Twenty-First Century, Scientific American, September 1991, pp.94–100,
• Wenzel, Jörg (2009), Das induktive Prinzip, Elektroniknet.de , Februar 2009, www.elektroniknet.de/home/automation/fachwissen/uebersicht/fedlebene/feldbusseethernetwireless/das-induktive-prinzip, downloaded on April 26th, 2009
• Wessel, Rhea (2008), German Institute tests RFID in Construction, RFID Journal, November 2008. www.rfidjournal.com/article/articleview/4468/1/1/, downloaded on April 26th, 2009
• Wiener, Oswald (1990), Probleme der künstlichen Intelligenz, ed. von Peter Weibel, Berlin: Merve
• Wiscombe, Tom (2009), Emergent Architecture: Bioconstructivsm, L'Arca 244, February 2009, p.43
• Woebken, Chris (2009), Sensual Interfaces, Archistorm Magazine, 01/2009
• Wymann, Jean-Pierre (2004), Wasserdurchströmtes Glas: Interview mit Dietrich Schwarz, TEC21 Fachzeitschrift für Architektur, Ingenieurwesen and Umwelt, pp.14–17
• Zimmermann, Gregor; Grohmann, Manfred (2008), Membrane concrete grid shells—pneumatic formwork: Ultra High Performance Concrete (UHPC), In Proceedings of the Second International Symposium on Ultra High Performance Concrete Kassel, Germany. March 05–07
• Zimmermann, Gregor; Grohmann, Manfred; Tessmann, Oliver; Schein, Markus (2007), In:Ex:terior Structures: Entwurf eines UHPC Pavillon, Kassel: Books On Demand
• Zottl, Susanne (2009), A Styrofoam Lover with (E)Motions of Concrete, Beton Zement 1/2009.

PICTURE CREDITS

INDEX

Editor: Thorsten Klooster
Authors: Niels Boeing (Nano, pp. 68–84), Simon Davis (Energy, pp. 85–100), Thorsten Klooster (Introduction, pp. 6–9;
Surfaces, pp. 62–67; Nano, pp. 68–84; Climate, pp. 116–130; Information, pp. 131–153), Almut Seeger (Light, pp. 101–115)

Graphic design, layout, illustration and cover design: onlab, Nicolas Bourquin, Maike Hamacher,
Barbara Hoffmann, Matthias Hübner, Marte Meling Enoksen, Thibaud Tissot, Judith Wimmer

Translation into English: Dr. Yasmin Gründing, Burglengenfeld/GER, Translation bureau Antoinette Aichele-Platen, Munich/GER
English copy editing: Richard Toovey, Berlin
Picture research: Markus Böke, Pauline Fer, Anni Hübner, Philipp Thole
Digital image processing: Steeg Digitaltechnik

Library of Congress Control Number: 2009925058
Bibliographic information published by the German National Library
The German National Library lists this publication in the Deutsche Nationalbibliografie; detailed bibliographic data are available on the
Internet at http://dnb.d-nb.de.

This book is also available in a German language edition (ISBN 978-3-7643-8811-9).

© 2009 Birkhäuser Verlag AG
Basel · Boston · Berlin
P.O. Box 133, CH-4010 Basel, Switzerland
Part of Springer Science+Business Media

Printed on acid-free paper produced from chlorine-free pulp. TCF ∞
Printed in Germany

ISBN 978-3-7643-8812-6

9 8 7 6 5 4 3 2 1
www.birkhauser.ch

My thanks are due to all of the architects, designers, artists, scientists and scientific institutions, as well as the firms named, that have
given me generous assistance with this book, in the form of texts, suggestions and illustrative material.

I am particularly grateful to:
Prof. Axel Oestreich and Andrea Wiegelmann for the idea for this book and their support in developing it;
Jan K. Knapp, Prof. Dr. Winfried Blau (Dresden), Prof. Dr. Hartmut Hillmer (Kassel), Helga Förster (Berlin), Prof. Heike Klussmann
(Kassel) and Sebastian Finckh for their expert advice and discussions with me;
Frank Möller (PI Ceramic GmbH), Andreas Häger and Thorsten Ronge (Inventux Technologies AG) and Oliver Wiesener,
Schneider Variolight GmbH for their specialist contributions;
Eileen Eckart, Prof. Peter A. Herms, Michele Sbrissa with Frammenti, Oliver Koerner von Gustorf, Frank Müller, Martin Permantier,
Ole Arand and Michael Schirner, who have all played similarly important parts in creating this book;
and especially to Maria Morais for her assessment at critical points and for her advice and patience day after day.